CLYMER™

YAMAHA

250-400cc PISTON-PORT • 1968-1976

The world's finest publisher of mechanical how-to manuals

INTERTEC PUBLISHING

P.O. Box 12901, Overland Park, Kansas 66282-2901

Copyright ©1981 Intertec Publishing Corporation

FIRST EDITION
First Printing January, 1977
Second Printing July, 1977

SECOND EDITION
First Printing August, 1977
Second Printing January, 1978

THIRD EDITION
First Printing June, 1978
Second Printing April, 1979
Third Printing May, 1980

FOURTH EDITION
First Printing April, 1981
Second Printing October, 1983
Third Printing July, 1985
Fourth Printing July, 1990
Fifth Printing March, 1993
Sixth Printing January, 1995
Seventh Printing August, 1997

Printed in U.S.A.

ISBN: 0-89287-276-4

MEMBER

COVER: Photographed by Michael Brown Photographic Productions, Los Angeles, California.

INTERTEC BOOKS

President and CEO Raymond E. Maloney
Vice President, Book Group Ted Marcus

The following books and guides are published by Intertec Publishing.

CLYMER SHOP MANUALS
Boat Motors and Drives
Motorcycles and ATVs
Snowmobiles
Personal Watercraft

ABOS/INTERTEC/CLYMER BLUE BOOKS AND TRADE-IN GUIDES
Recreational Vehicles
Outdoor Power Equipment
Agricultural Tractors
Lawn and Garden Tractors
Motorcycles and ATVs
Snowmobiles and Personal Watercraft
Boats and Motors

AIRCRAFT BLUEBOOK-PRICE DIGEST
Airplanes
Helicopters

AC-U-KWIK DIRECTORIES
The Corporate Pilot's Airport/FBO Directory
International Manager's Edition
Jet Book

I&T SHOP SERVICE MANUALS
Tractors

INTERTEC SERVICE MANUALS
Snowmobiles
Outdoor Power Equipment
Personal Watercraft
Gasoline and Diesel Engines
Recreational Vehicles
Boat Motors and Drives
Motorcycles
Lawn and Garden Tractors

CONTENTS

QUICK REFERENCE DATA

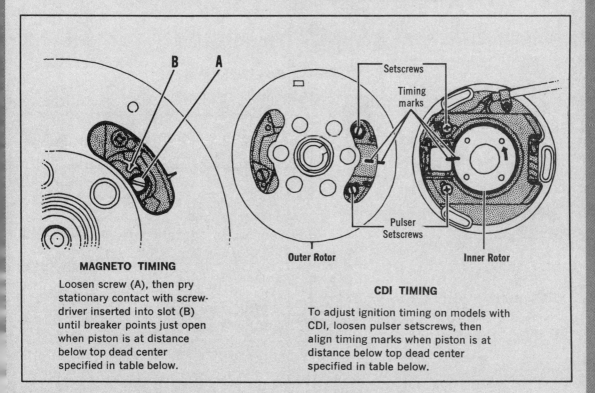

MAGNETO TIMING

Loosen screw (A), then pry stationary contact with screwdriver inserted into slot (B) until breaker points just open when piston is at distance below top dead center specified in table below.

CDI TIMING

To adjust ignition timing on models with CDI, loosen pulser setscrews, then align timing marks when piston is at distance below top dead center specified in table below.

ENGINE TUNE-UP

Model	Spark Plug		Spark plug gap (Inch)	Ignition Timing	
	NGK	ND		Inch	mm
DT1, DT1B	B7E		0.024	0.126	3.2
DT1C, DT1E	B8ES	W24ES	0.024	0.126	3.2
DT2, DT3	B8ES	W24ES	0.024	0.126*	3.2*
DT1C-MX, DT1E-MX	B10EN	W31EN	0.024	0.091	2.3
DT2-MX	B9EV	W27ESG	0.024	0.091*	2.3*
MX250	B8EV	W24ESG	0.024	0.091	2.3
YZ250	B8EV	W24ESG	0.016	0.091	2.3
DT250	B8ES	W24ES	0.024	0.126	3.2
RT1, RT1-B	B9ES	W27ES	0.024	0.114*	2.9*
RT1-MX, RT1B-MX	B9EN	W27EN	0.024	0.114	2.9
RT2, RT3	B9ES	W27ES	0.024	0.114	2.9
RT2-MX	B9EV	W27ESG	0.024	0.098	2.5
DT360	B9ES	W27ES	0.024	0.114	2.9
MX360	B8EV	W24ESG	0.016	0.098	2.5
YZ360	B8EV	W24ESG	0.016	0.091	2.3
DT400	B9ES	W27ES	0.024	0.106	2.7

Lever in RETARDED position

Lever in ADVANCED position

Wedge lever in full advance position when setting timing.

*See drawing

NOTE: On models with magneto ignition, point gap adjustment is not required, except for that which is made to adjust ignition timing.

FORK OIL QUANTITY

Model	Oil Quantity*	
	Ounces	Milliliters
DT1, -B, -C	7.1	210
DT1-E, DT1E-MX	5.9	175
DT2, -MX	5.9	175
DT3, MX250, DT250	5.9	175
MX250A, YZ250	6.6	195
RT1, -MX	7.1	210
RT1B, -MX	5.9	175
RT2, -MX	5.9	175
RT3	5.9	175
MX360	6.6	195
YZ360	6.6	195
YZ400	14.1	415

*SAE 10W-30. Use SAE 30 or 40 for hot weather or severe use.

STANDARD TIGHTENING TORQUE

Fastener Size (Millimeters)		Tightening Torque	
		Ft.-lb.	Mkg
Bolt	Nut		
6	10	7.2	1.0
8	13	15	2.0
8	14	15	2.0
10	17	25-29	3.5-4.0
12	19	29-33	4.0-4.5
14	22	33-36	4.5-5.0
17	26	43-51	6.0-7.0
18	27	43-51	6.0-7.0
20	30	51-58	7.0-8.0
Spark plug		18-22	2.5-3.0

ADJUSTMENT

Front brake lever clearance	$\frac{3}{16}$-$\frac{5}{16}$ in. (5-8mm)
Rear brake pedal free play	1 in. (25mm)
Clutch lever clearance	$\frac{1}{16}$-$\frac{1}{8}$ in. (2-3mm)
Drive chain play	$\frac{3}{4}$-1 in. (19-25mm)

TIRES

	Front	Rear
Tire pressure (psi)		
Road	13	16
Trail	8.5	10
Tire size		
DT1, DT1B DT1-C, DT1-E DT2, DT3 RT1, RT1-B RT2, RT3	3.25x19	4.00x18
DT1-MX DT1C-MX RT1-MX	2.75x21	4.00x18
DT2-MX MX250 YZ250A	3.00x21	4.00x18
RT2-MX DT250 MX360 DT360 DT400	3.00x21	4.00x18
YZ360A	3.00x21	4.60x18

TRANSMISSION OIL QUANTITY*

Engine Size	Quantity	
250 (through 1973)	34 ounces	1,000 milliliters
250 (1974 and later)	41 ounces	1,200 milliliters
360 (1974 and later)	41 ounces	1,200 milliliters
400	34 ounces	1,000 milliliters

*SAE 10W-30 engine oil.

CHAPTER ONE

GENERAL INFORMATION

This manual provides service information and procedures for Yamaha 250-400 cc single cylinder, 2-stroke motorcycles built for the U.S. market from 1968-on.

MANUAL ORGANIZATION

All dimensions and capacities are expressed in English units familiar to U.S. mechanics as well as in metric units. *Metric tools are required to work on Yamahas.*

This chapter provides general information, service hints, and tool recommendations.

Chapter Two describes all periodic lubrication and periodic maintenance necessary to keep your bike running well. Recommended tune-up procedures are also included in this chapter.

Troubleshooting procedures are located in Chapter Three. These procedures provide methods and suggestions for quick and accurate diagonsis and repair of problems. These procedures discuss typical symptoms and logical methods to pinpoint the trouble.

Subsequent chapters cover specific systems such as the engine, transmission, and electrical systems. Each of these chapters provides disassembly, repair, and assembly procedures in simple step-by-step format. If a repair requires special skills or tools, or is otherwise impractical for the home mechanic, it is so indicated. In these cases it is usually faster and less expensive to have the repairs made by a Honda dealer or competent repair shop. Necessary specifications concerning a particular system are included at the end of the appropriate chapter.

When special tools are required to perform a procedure included in this manual, the tool is illustrated either in actual use or alone. It may be possible to rent or borrow these tools. The inventive mechanic may also be able to find a suitable substitute in his tool box or to fabricate one.

The terms NOTE, CAUTION, and WARNING have specific meanings in this manual. A NOTE provides additional or explanatory information. A CAUTION is used to emphasize areas where equipment damage could result if proper precautions are not taken. A WARNING is used to stress those areas where personal damage or death could result from negligence, in addition to possible mechanical damage.

In using the procedures in this manual, bear in mind that "front" refers to the front of the bike, and that "right" and "left" means the right and left sides of the motorcycle as viewed from the seat, facing the front, in the riding position.

The front of a component is that end which faces to the front of the bike. These rules are simple, but even experienced mechanics occasionally become disoriented.

SERVICE HINTS

Most of the service procedures described in this book are straightforward, and can be performed by anyone who is reasonably handy with tools. However, consider your own capabilities carefully before attempting any operation which involves major engine disassembly.

Crankshaft overhaul, for example, requires a press, precision test fixtures, and considerable experience. It would be wiser to have that operation performed by a shop equipped for such work, rather than to try it with makeshift equipment. Other procedures require precision measurements. Unless you have the skills and equipment to make these measurements, call on a competent service shop.

Repairs go much faster and easier if your machine is clean before you begin work. There are special cleaners for washing the engine and related parts. You just brush or spray on the cleaning solution, let it stand, and rinse it away with a garden hose. Clean all oily or greasy parts with cleaning solvent as you remove them. *Never use gasoline as a cleaning agent.* Gasoline presents an extreme fire hazard. Be sure to work in a well ventilated area when you use cleaning solvent. Keep a fire extinguisher handy, just in case.

Special tools are required for some service procedures. These tools may be purchased at Yamaha dealers. If you are on good terms with the dealer's service department, you may be able to use his.

Much of the labor charge for repairs made by dealers is for removal and disassembly of other parts to reach the defective one. It is frequently possible for you to do all of this yourself, then take the affected subassembly, such as the crankshaft mentioned earlier, into the dealer for repair.

Once you decide to tackle the job yourself, read the entire section in this manual which pertains to the job. Study the illustrations and the text until you have a good idea of what is involved. If special tools are required, make

arrangements to get them before you start the job. It is frustrating to get partly into a job and find that you are unable to complete it.

TOOLS

Every motorcyclist should carry a small tool kit with him, to help make minor roadside adjustments and repairs. A suggested kit, available at most dealers, is shown in **Figure 1**.

For more extensive servicing, an assortment of ordinary hand tools is required. As a minimum, have the following available. Note that all threaded fasteners are metric sizes.

1. Combination wrenches
2. Socket wrenches
3. Assorted screwdrivers
4. Assorted pliers
5. Spark plug gauge
6. Spark plug wrench
7. Small hammer
8. Plastic and rubber mallet
9. Parts cleaning brush

A few special tools may also be required. The first four are essential.

1. *Flywheel puller* (**Figure 2**). Yamaha bikes with magnetos require that the flywheel be removed to gain access to the breaker points. This tool costs around $6, and it is available at most motorcycle shops or by mail order from accessory dealers. Be sure to specify the model of your machine when ordering. There is no satisfactory substitute for this tool; but there have been many unhappy owners who bought expensive new crankshafts and flywheels after trying makeshift flywheel removal methods.

2. *Ignition gauge* (**Figure 3**). This tool combines round wire spark plug gauges with narrow

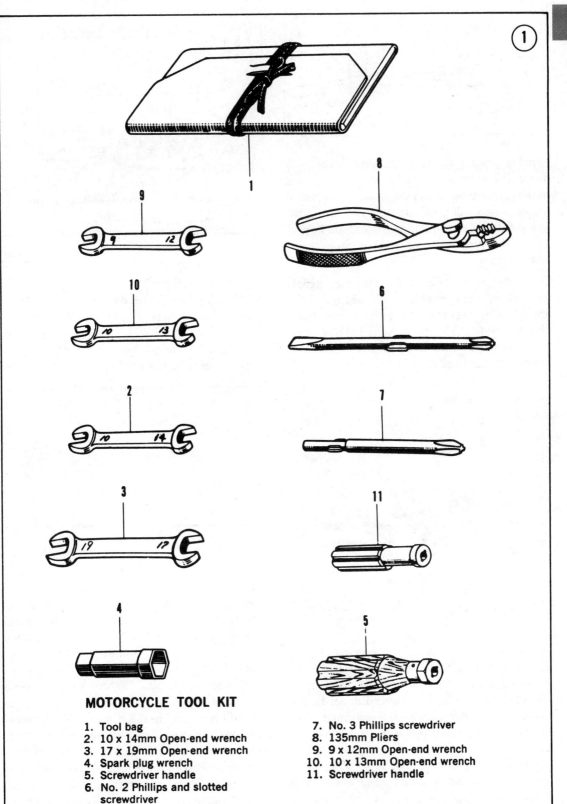

MOTORCYCLE TOOL KIT

1. Tool bag
2. 10 x 14mm Open-end wrench
3. 17 x 19mm Open-end wrench
4. Spark plug wrench
5. Screwdriver handle
6. No. 2 Phillips and slotted screwdriver
7. No. 3 Phillips screwdriver
8. 135mm Pliers
9. 9 x 12mm Open-end wrench
10. 10 x 13mm Open-end wrench
11. Screwdriver handle

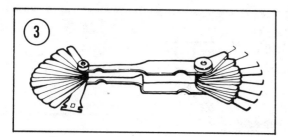

breaker point feeler gauges. Most bikes with magnetos require that point gap be adjusted through a narrow slot in the flywheel. Standard feeler gauges will not fit through this slot, making point gap measurement difficult or impossible. This tool costs about $3 at auto accessory stores.

3. *Timing tester* (**Figure 4**). This unit signals the instant when breaker points just open. On models with magnetos, this point is sometimes difficult to determine with a test light or ohmmeter, because the breaker points are shunted by a low-resistance coil.

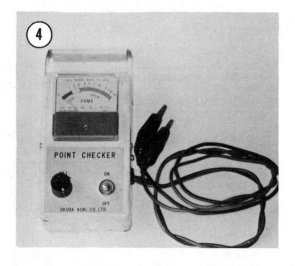

4. *Timing gauge* (**Figure 5**). Yamaha bikes require that ignition timing be set by adjusting the breaker points so that they just begin to open when the piston is at a specified distance below top dead center. By screwing this instrument into the spark plug hole, piston position may be determined.

The tool shown is priced at about $20, and is available from larger dealers and mail order houses. Less expensive ones, which utilize a vernier scale instead of a dial indicator, are also

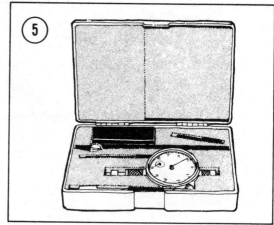

available. They are also satisfactory, but not quite so quick and easy to use.

5. *Hydrometer* (**Figure 6**). This tool measures charge of the battery, and tells much about battery condition. Available at any auto parts store and through most mail order outlets, a typical hydrometer costs less than $3.

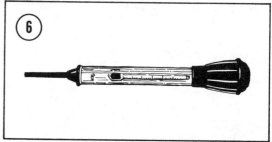

6. *Multimeter, or VOM* (**Figure 7**). This instrument is invaluable for electrical system troubleshooting and service. A few of its functions may be duplicated by locally fabricated substitutes, but for the serious hobbyist, it is a must. Its uses are described in the applicable sections of this book. Prices start at around $10 at electronics hobbyist stores and mail order outlets.

7. *Compression gauge* (**Figure 8**). An engine with low compression cannot be properly tuned and will not develop full power. The compression gauge shown has a flexible stem, which enables it to reach cylinders where there is little clearance between the cylinder head and frame. Less expensive gauges start at around $3, and are available at auto accessory stores or by mail order.

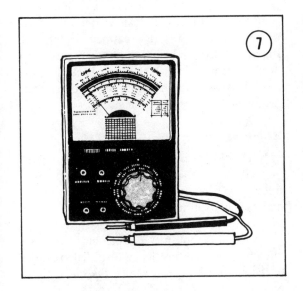

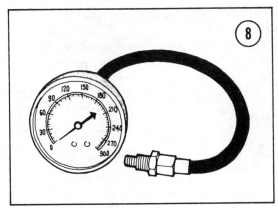

8. *Impact driver* (**Figure 9**). This tool might have been designed with the motorcyclist in mind. It makes removal of engine cover screws easy, and eliminates damaged screw slots. Good ones run about $12 at larger hardware stores.

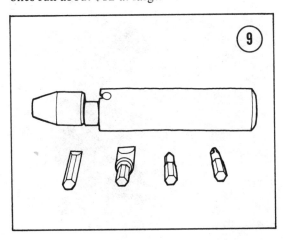

EXPENDABLE SUPPLIES

Certain expendable supplies are also required. These include grease, oil, gasket cement, wiping rags, cleaning solvent, and distilled water. Cleaning solvent is available at many service stations. Distilled water, required for battery service, is available at every supermarket. It is sold for use in steam irons, and is quite inexpensive.

MECHANIC'S TIPS

Removing Frozen Nuts and Screws

When a fastener rusts and cannot be removed, several methods may be used to loosen it. First, apply penetrating oil liberally, then rap the fastener with a small hammer. Do not hit it hard enough to cause damage.

For frozen screws, apply oil as described, then insert a screwdriver in the slot and rap the top of the screwdriver with a hammer. This loosens the rust so the screw can be removed in the normal way. If the screw head is too chewed up to use a screwdriver, grip the head with vise-type pliers and turn the screw out.

For a frozen bolt or nut, apply penetrating oil, than rap it with a hammer. Turn off with the proper size wrench. If the points are rounded off, grip with vise-type pliers as described for screws.

Stripped Threads

Occasionally, threads are stripped through carelessness or impact damage. Often the threads can be cleaned up by running a tap (for internal threads) or die (for external threads) through the threads. See **Figure 10**.

Broken Screw or Bolt

When the head breaks off a screw or bolt, several methods are available for removing the remaining portion.

If a large portion of the remainder projects out, try gripping it with vise-type pliers. If the projecting portion is too small, try filing it to fit a wrench or cut a slot in it to fit a screwdriver. See **Figure 11**.

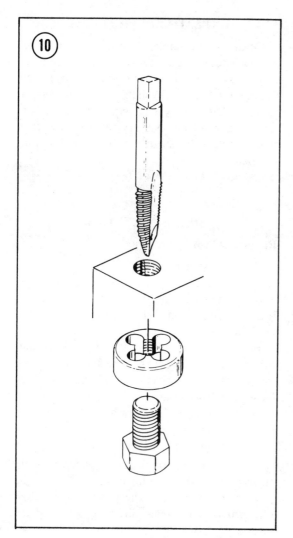

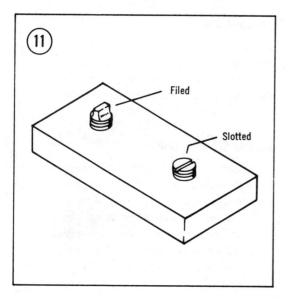

Filed

Slotted

If the head breaks off flush, as it usually does, remove it with a screw extractor. Refer to **Figure 12**. Center-punch the broken part, then drill a hole into it. Drill sizes are marked on the tool. Tap the extractor into the broken part, then back it out with a wrench.

Removing Frozen Nuts

Nuts subject to corrosion or high temperatures, such as those which retain exhaust pipes, frequently become impossible to remove normally. A nut splitter is an invaluable tool under such circumstances.

To use this tool, merely position it over the offending nut and turn its cutting blade parallel to the stud or bolt from which the nut is to be removed (**Figure 13**). Then turn the pressure screw on the tool until the nut splits (**Figure 14**). Internal forces in the nut will cause it to loosen from the stud so that it may be removed easily. The stud will be undamaged by this procedure.

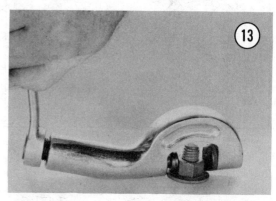

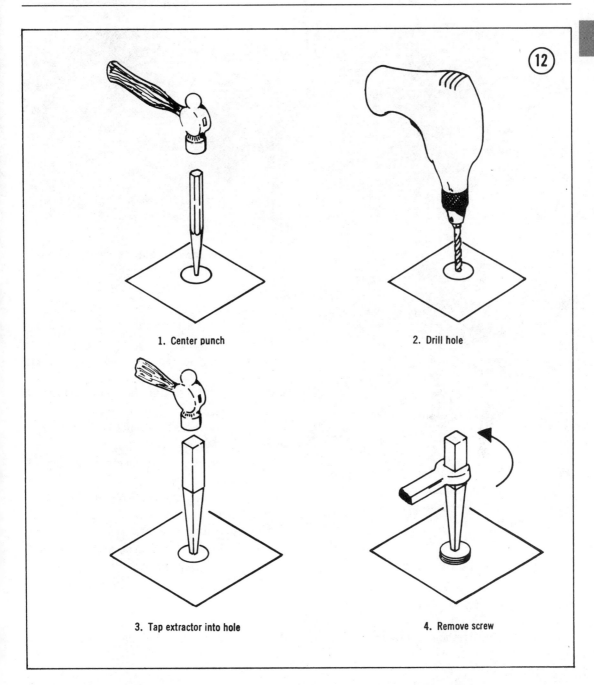

1. Center punch

2. Drill hole

3. Tap extractor into hole

4. Remove screw

Removing Damaged Screws

> WARNING
> *When removing screws by this method, always wear suitable eye protection.*

> CAUTION
> *Use clean rags to cover bearings or any other parts which might be harmed by metal chips produced during this procedure.*

Figure 15 illustrates damaged screws typical of those on many bikes. Such screws may usually be removed easily by drilling. Select a bit with a diameter larger than that of the damaged screw, but smaller than its head, then drill into the screw head (**Figure 16**) until the head separates from the screw. The remainder of the screw may then be turned out easily. **Figure 17** illustrates one screw head removed in this man-

ner. The other has been drilled to just the point where the head is separating from the screw body. Note that there is no damage to the plate which these screws retain.

SAFETY FIRST

Professional mechanics can work for years without sustaining serious injury. If you observe a few rules of common sense and safety, you can also enjoy many safe hours servicing your own

machine. You can also hurt yourself or damage the bike if you ignore these rules.

1. Never use gasoline as a cleaning solvent.

2. Never smoke or use a torch near flammable liquids, such as cleaning solvent in open containers.

3. Never smoke or use a torch in an area where batteries are charging. Highly explosive hydrogen gas is formed during the charging process.

4. If welding or brazing is required on the machine, remove the fuel tank to a safe distance, at least 50 feet away.

5. Be sure to use the proper size wrench for turning nuts.

6. If a nut is tight, think for a moment what would happen to your hand should the wrench slip. Be guided accordingly.

7. Keep your work area clean and uncluttered.

8. Wear safety goggles for all operations involving drilling, grinding, or use of a chisel.

9. Never use worn tools.

10. Keep a fire extinguisher handy. Be sure that it is rated for gasoline and electrical fires.

CHAPTER TWO

PERIODIC MAINTENANCE

To gain the utmost in safety, performance, and useful life from your motorcycle, it is necessary to make periodic inspections and adjustments. It frequently happens that minor problems found during such inspections are simple and inexpensive to correct at the time, but could lead to major failures later. This chapter describes such services.

Table 1 is a suggested maintenance schedule.

Table 1   MAINTENANCE SCHEDULE

Maintenance Item	Initial 500 Miles	Every 1,000 Miles	Every 2,000 Miles
Check spark plug	X	X	
Engine tune-up			X
Adjust clutch	X	X	
Adjust brakes	X	X	
Check wheels	X	X	
Service chain	X	X	
Check battery	X	X	
Check electrical equipment	X	X	
Tighten all fasteners			X
Clean exhaust system			X

ENGINE TUNE-UP

The number of definitions of the term "tune-up" is probably equal to the number of people defining it. For purposes of this book, we will define a tune-up as a general adjustment and/or maintenance of all service items to ensure continued peak operating efficiency of a motorcycle engine.

As part of a proper tune-up, some service operations are essential. The following paragraphs discuss details of these procedures. Service operations should be performed in the order specified. Unless otherwise specified, the engine should be thoroughly cool before starting any tune-up service.

Spark Plug

As the first step in any tune-up, remove and examine the spark plug, because spark plug condition can tell much about engine condition and carburetor adjustment.

To remove the spark plug, first clean the area around its base to prevent dirt or other foreign material from entering the cylinder. Then unscrew the spark plug, using a suitable deep socket. If difficulty is encountered removing a spark plug, apply penetrating oil to its base and allow some 20 minutes for the oil to work in. It may also be helpful to rap the cylinder head lightly with a rubber or plastic mallet; this procedure sets up vibrations which help the penetrating oil to work in. Be careful not to break any cooling fins when tapping the cylinder head.

Figure 1 illustrates various conditions which might be encountered upon plug removal.

Normal condition—If plugs have a light tan or gray colored deposit and no abnormal gap wear or erosion, good engine, carburetion, and ignition condition are indicated. The plug in use is of the proper heat range, and may be serviced and returned to use.

Carbon fouled—Soft, dry sooty deposits are evidence of incomplete combustion and can usually be attributed to rich carburetion. The condition is also sometimes caused by weak ignition, retarded ignition timing, or low compression. Such a plug may usually be cleaned and returned to service, but the condition which causes fouling should be corrected.

Oil fouled—This plug exhibits a black insulator tip, damp, oily film over the firing end, and a carbon layer over the entire nose. Electrodes will not be worn. Common causes for this condition are listed below:

  a. Improper fuel/oil mixture
  b. Wrong type of oil
  c. Idle speed too low
  d. Idle mixture too rich
  e. Clogged air filter
  f. Weak ignition
  g. Excessive idling
  h. Autolube pump out of adjustment
  i. Wrong spark plugs (too cold)

Oil fouled spark plugs may be cleaned in a pinch, but it is better to replace them. It is important to correct the cause of fouling before the engine is returned to service.

Gap bridging—Plugs with this condition exhibit gaps shorted out by combustion chamber deposits fused between electrodes. Any of the following may be the cause:

  a. Improper fuel/oil mixture
  b. Clogged exhaust
  c. Autolube pump misadjusted

Be sure to locate and correct the cause of this spark plug condition. Such plugs must be replaced with new ones.

Overheated—Overheated spark plugs exhibit burned electrodes. The insulator tip will be light gray or even chalk white. The most common cause for this condition is use of a spark plug of the wrong heat range (too hot). If it is known that the correct plug is used, other causes are lean fuel mixture, engine overloading or lugging, loose carburetor mounting, or overadvanced ignition timing. Always correct the fault before putting the bike back into service. Such plugs cannot be salvaged; replace them with new ones.

Worn out—Corrosive gases formed by combustion and high voltage sparks have eroded the electrodes. Spark plugs in this condition require more voltage to fire under hard acceleration; often more than the ignition system can supply. Replace them with new plugs of the same heat range.

Preignition—If electrodes are melted, preignition is almost certainly the cause. Check for loose carburetor mounting or overadvanced ignition timing. It is also possible that a plug of the wrong heat range (too hot) is being used. Find the cause of preignition before placing the engine back into service.

Spark plugs may usually be cleaned and regapped, which will restore them to near-new condition. Since the effort involved is considerable, such service may not be worth it, since new spark plugs are relatively inexpensive.

For those who wish to service used plugs, use the following procedure.

1. Clean all oily deposits from the spark plug with cleaning solvent, then blow dry with compressed air. Oily deposits cause gumming or caking of the sandblast cleaner.

2. Place the spark plug in a sandblast cleaner and blast 3-5 seconds, then turn on air only to remove particles from the plug.

SPARK PLUG CONDITIONS ①

NORMAL USE

OIL FOULED

CARBON FOULED

OVERHEATED

GAP BRIDGED

SUSTAINED PREIGNITION

WORN OUT

Photos courtesy of Champion Spark Plug Company.

2

3. Repeat Step 2 as required until the plug is cleaned. Prolonged sandblasting will erode the insulator and make the plug more susceptible to fouling.

4. Bend the side electrode up slightly, then file the center electrode so that its edges are not rounded. Less voltage is required to jump between sharp corners than between rounded edges.

5. Adjust spark plug gap to 0.024 in. (0.6mm) for all models. Use a round wire gauge for measurement (**Figure 2**). Always adjust spark plug gap by bending the outer electrode only. A spark plug gapping tool does the best job, if one is available.

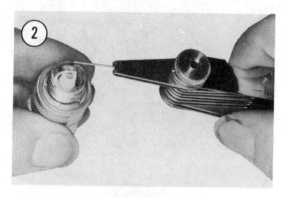

It will be easier to turn the crankshaft over for other service operations if you leave the spark plug out until it is time to start the engine. Torque spark plugs to 18-22 ft.-lb. (2.5-3.0 mkg) upon installation.

Compression Test

An engine requires adequate compression to develop full power. A compression test, or even better, a series of them over the life of the bike, will tell much about engine condition.

To make a compression test, proceed as follows.

1. Start the engine, then ride the bike long enough to warm it thoroughly.

2. Remove the spark plug.

3. Screw the compression gauge into the spark plug hole, or if a press-in type gauge is used, hold it firmly in position.

4. With the ignition switch OFF and the throttle fully open, crank the engine briskly with the

kickstarter several times; the compression gauge indication will increase with each kick. Continue to crank the engine until the gauge shows no more increase, then record the gauge indication.

Because of differences in engine design, carbon deposits, and other factors, no definite compression readings can be specified for any one engine. Typical compression pressures will range from 100-150 psi.

A series of measurements made over a period of time may reveal an indication of trouble ahead, long before the engine exhibits serious symptoms. A difference of 20 percent between successive readings over a period of time is an indication of trouble.

Note that a one-time compression test made at 8,000 miles might be considered normal, but compared with the engine's past history, it could indicate trouble. A permanent record of compression tests must be done with the same gauge. Measurements taken with different gauges are not necessarily conclusive, because of production tolerances, calibration errors, and other factors.

Carbon Removal

Two-stroke engines are particularly susceptible to carbon formation. Deposits form on the inside of the cylinder head, on top of the piston, and within the exhaust port. Combustion chamber deposits can abnormally increase compression ratio, causing overheating, preignition, and possible severe engine damage. Carbon deposits within the exhaust port, exhaust pipe, and muffler restrict engine breathing, causing loss of power. To remove carbon from the engine, it is necessary to first remove the cylinder head. It is usually unnecessary to remove the piston. Always allow the engine to cool to avoid possible cylinder head warpage. To remove the cylinder head, proceed as follows.

1. Remove the spark plug.

2. On models with four 8mm and four 10mm cylinder head nuts, loosen each 8mm nut a quarter turn at a time in a crisscross sequence until each turns freely. Then repeat for the four 10mm nuts. On other models, loosen each nut in a crisscross sequence until each turns

freely, then remove all nuts. This procedure minimizes chances for cylinder head warpage.

3. Lift the cylinder head from the cylinder (**Figure 3**). If it sticks, tap it lightly with a rubber mallet. Do not pry it off; doing so may cause damage to sealing surfaces.

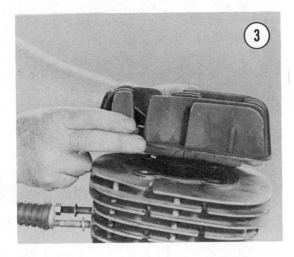

4. Reverse the removal procedure to install the head. Always use a new cylinder head gasket. Torque cylinder head nuts in 3 progressive stages to the values specified in **Table 2**. Tighten the 10mm nuts first.

Table 2   CYLINDER HEAD NUT TORQUE

Model	Torque	
	Ft.-lb.	Mkg
250-360		
8mm nuts	15-18	2.0-2.5
10mm nuts	25-30	3.5-4.0
400		
13mm nuts	15	2.0
17mm nuts	25	3.5
500		
8mm nuts	15-18	2.0-2.5
10mm nuts	25-30	3.5-4.0
Note: Tighten larger nuts first.		

An easy method for removing cylinder head deposits is to use the rounded end of a hacksaw blade as a scraper, as shown in **Figure 4**. Be very careful not to cause any damage to the sealing surface.

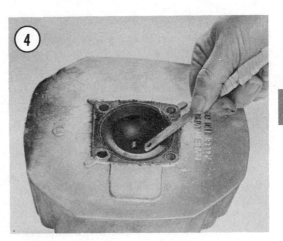

The same tool may be used for removing carbon deposits from piston heads (**Figure 5**). After removing all deposits from the piston head, clean all carbon and gum from the piston ring grooves using a ring groove cleaning tool or broken piston ring (**Figure 6**). Any deposits left in the grooves will cause the piston rings to stick, thereby causing gas blow-by and loss of power.

To remove piston rings, it is only necessary to spread the top ring with a thumb on each end (**Figure 7**), then remove it upward. Repeat the procedure for each remaining ring. When replacing the rings, be sure that the ends of the rings engage the locating pins in the grooves (**Figure 8**).

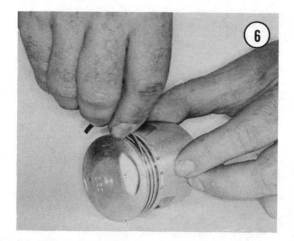

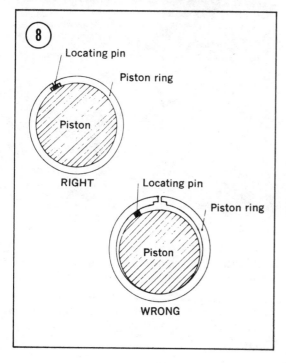

Remove the oil pump output tube (**Figure 9**) from the lower right side of the cylinder. On models so equipped, loosen the cylinder base in crisscross order and remove the nuts also. Tap the cylinder lightly at the intake and exhaust ports to loosen it, then lift it from the crankcase (**Figure 10**). Stuff clean rags into the crankcase opening to prevent entry of foreign material.

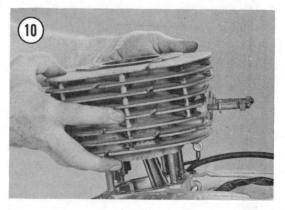

Scrape all carbon deposits from the cylinder exhaust port, as shown in **Figure 11**. A blunted screwdriver is a suitable tool for this job.

Reverse the removal procedure to install the cylinder. Tighten cylinder base nuts to 25-29 ft.-lb. (3.5-4.0 mkg) in crisscross order, in 3 progressive steps. Be sure to lubricate the piston and cylinder liberally before installation. Note that when installing the cylinder, it is necessary to compress each piston ring as it enters the cylinder. A ring compressor tool makes the job easier, but the rings may be compressed by hand with little difficulty.

Breaker Points

Normal use of a motorcycle causes the breaker points to burn and pit gradually. If they are not too pitted, they can be dressed with a few strokes of a clean point file. Do not use emery cloth or sandpaper, because particles can remain on the points and cause arcing and burning. If a few strokes of a file do not smooth the points completely, replace them.

Oil or dirt may get on the points, resulting in poor performance or even premature failure. Common causes for this condition are defective oil seals, improper or excessive breaker cam lubrication, or lack of care when the breaker point cover is removed.

Points should be cleaned and regapped approximately every 1,500-2,000 miles (2,000-3,000 kilometers). To clean the points, first dress them lightly with a clean point file, then remove all residue with lacquer thinner. Close the points on a piece of clean white paper such as a business card. Continue to pull the card through the closed points until no discoloration or residue remains on the card. Finally, rotate the engine and observe the points as they open and close. If they do not meet squarely, replace them.

If poor engine performance has been traced to oil-fouled points, correct the cause before returning the motorcycle to service.

To service or replace breaker points on models with magneto ignition, proceed as follows.

1. Remove gearshift lever. The clamping bolt must be removed completely before the lever can be pulled from the shaft.

2. Remove left crankshaft cover. An impact driver makes it easy to loosen the cover screws without damaging them.

3. Remove flywheel retaining nut and lockwasher.

4. Screw a flywheel puller (left-hand thread) into the flywheel to its full depth. Be sure that the puller screw is backed out fully when installing the puller. Turn the puller screw clockwise to remove the flywheel (**Figure 12**).

5. Remove the wire, then remove point retaining screw (A, **Figure 13**).

6. After the new points are installed, tighten screw (A) just enough so that the stationary contact does not slip, but not so much that the contact cannot be moved by a screwdriver twisted in pry slots (B). Move the stationary contact until both points just barely make contact.

7. Install flywheel, lockwasher, and flywheel retaining nut. Tighten flywheel retaining nut securely.

8. Adjust ignition timing.

Magneto Ignition Timing

1. Using a suitable adapter, mount a dial gauge so that piston position may be determined accurately (**Figure 14**). Adapters and retaining nuts are available at Yamaha dealers.

2. Turn engine until dial gauge indicates that piston is at top dead center. Set dial gauge to zero.

3. Turn the engine clockwise until the piston is about ¼ in. (6mm) below top dead center.

4. Connect a timing tester between the wire on the points and a good engine ground. Follow the tester manufacturer's instructions for connection.

5. Slowly turn engine counterclockwise until timing tester indicates that breaker points just open.

6. Observe dial gauge. If it indicates the distance specified in **Table 3**, no adjustment is required.

Table 3   MAGNETO IGNITION TIMING

| Model | Distance BTDC | |
	Inch	Millimeters
DT1, DT1B, DT1C, DT1E	0.126	3.2
DT1C-MX, DT1E-MX	0.091	2.3
DT2, DT3	0.126*	3.2*
DT2-MX	0.126	3.2
RT1, RT1-B	0.114*	2.9*
RT1-MX, RT1B-MX	0.114	2.9
RT2, RT3	0.114	2.9
RT2-MX	0.098	2.5

*Lever in full advance position

7. If adjustment is required, turn engine until piston is at distance specified in Table 3.

8. Refer to **Figure 15**. Slightly loosen screw (A), then insert a screwdriver into pry slots (B) to move stationary contact until breaker points just open.

NOTE: *Figure 15 shows flywheel removed for clarity. Adjust timing with flywheel in place.*

9. Tighten screw (A), then recheck and readjust if necessary.

CDI Timing

Some models are equipped with electronic ignition systems (CDI). These systems can be described as inner- or outer-rotor types, illustrated in **Figures 16 and 17**.

Once adjusted, ignition timing should not change, but it should be checked periodically. Ignition timing procedures are similar for both types of systems; differences are pointed out where they exist.

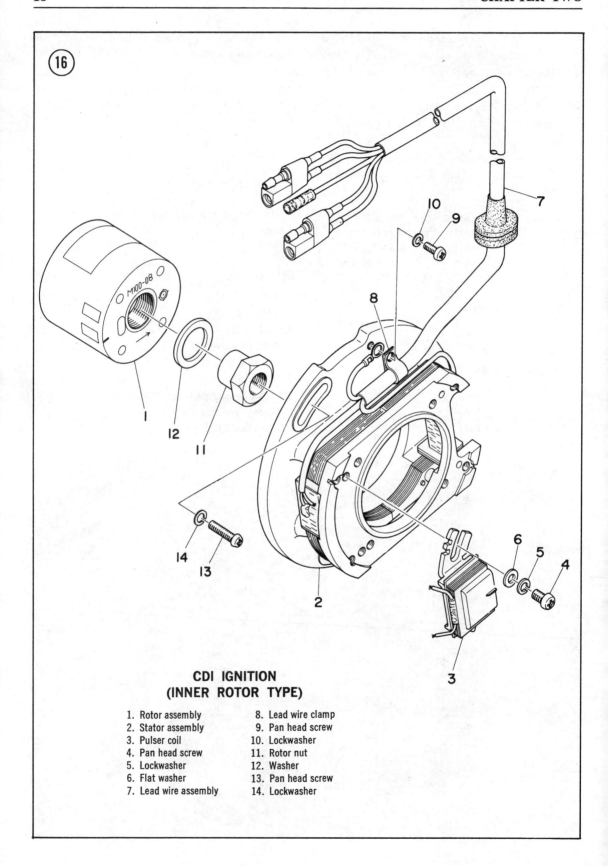

CDI IGNITION
(INNER ROTOR TYPE)

1. Rotor assembly
2. Stator assembly
3. Pulser coil
4. Pan head screw
5. Lockwasher
6. Flat washer
7. Lead wire assembly
8. Lead wire clamp
9. Pan head screw
10. Lockwasher
11. Rotor nut
12. Washer
13. Pan head screw
14. Lockwasher

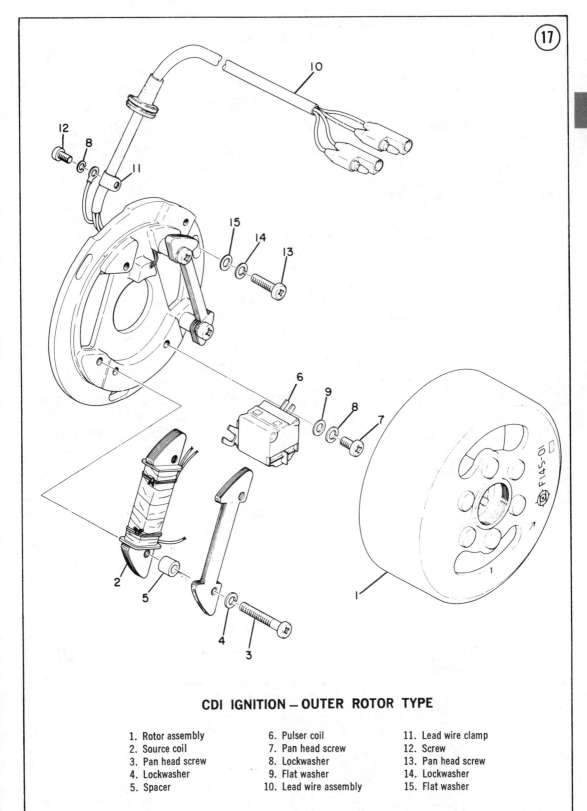

CDI IGNITION — OUTER ROTOR TYPE

1. Rotor assembly
2. Source coil
3. Pan head screw
4. Lockwasher
5. Spacer
6. Pulser coil
7. Pan head screw
8. Lockwasher
9. Flat washer
10. Lead wire assembly
11. Lead wire clamp
12. Screw
13. Pan head screw
14. Lockwasher
15. Flat washer

1. Remove cylinder head, then mount a dial gauge so that piston position may be determined accurately.

2. Rotate engine counterclockwise until piston is at top dead center. Zero the dial gauge.

3. Rotate engine clockwise until piston is at distance below top dead center specified in **Table 4**.

Table 4   CDI IGNITION TIMING

Model	Inch	(mm)
MX250	0.091	2.3
YZ250	0.091	2.3
RT2-MX	0.098	2.5
MX360	0.098	2.5
YZ360	0.091	2.3
DT400	0.106	2.7

4. Refer to **Figure 18 or 19** as applicable. Timing marks must align. If marks do not align, loosen pulser set screws slightly, then move pulser coil until alignment is achieved. Be sure to tighten both set screws.

5. Recheck ignition timing.

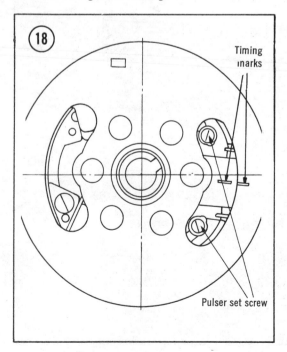

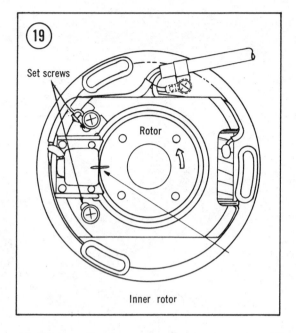

Set screws

Rotor

Inner rotor

Air Cleaner Service

As part of any tune-up, air cleaner elements should be cleaned or replaced, as required. A clogged air cleaner results in an overrich mixture, causing power loss and poor gas mileage. Be sure that the air cleaner element is not torn and that it fits so that no dirt can leak past its edges.

Replace air cleaner elements if they become torn, punctured, or so clogged that dirt cannot be removed.

Some models are equipped with polyurethane foam air cleaner elements. Wash such elements in solvent, dry thoroughly, then wet lightly but thoroughly with engine oil before installation. Replace the element if it is torn or punctured.

Fuel Strainer

Remove and clean the fuel strainer. Blow dry with compressed air. Be sure that the fuel petcock does not leak. Dirty fuel strainers are a major cause of carburetor flooding.

Carburetor Adjustment

Carburetor adjustment is the last step to be done on the engine, because it cannot be done accurately until all other adjustments are correct. The carburetor must also be adjusted with the engine thoroughly warmed, while most other

Timing marks

Pulser set screw

adjustments either must be or are more easily done with the engine cold.

Idle speed and idle mixture are normally the only carburetor adjustments performed at the time of engine tune-up. If other adjustments seem to be required, refer to Chapter Five for details of major carburetor service.

1. Turn in idle mixture screw (**Figure 20**) until it seats lightly, then back it out 1¼ turns.

2. Start engine, then ride bike long enough to warm it thoroughly.

3. Turn idle speed adjuster until engine runs slower and begins to falter.

4. Turn idle mixture screw as required to make the engine run smoothly.

5. Repeat Steps 3 and 4 to achieve the lowest stable idle speed.

6. Adjust final idle speed as desired.

Autolube Pump Adjustment

1. With engine not running, close throttle (engine idle position).

2. Rotate Autolube pump starter plate (**Figure 21**) in direction of arrow until plunger on forward end of pump moves outward to the end of its stroke.

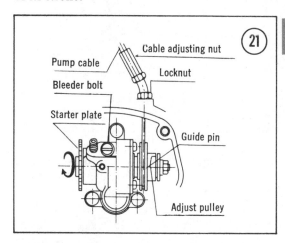

3. Measure gap between adjustment plate and raised portion of pump pulley (**Figure 22**). This gap should be 0.008-0.010 in. (0.20-0.25mm). Minimum allowable gap is 0.006 in. (0.15mm).

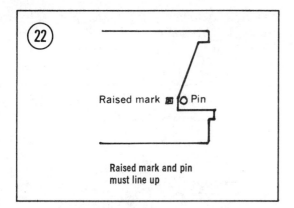

Raised mark and pin must line up

4. If adjustment is required, remove adjustment plate locknut, then adjustment plate. Add or remove shims under adjustment plate as necessary. Adding shims increases gap. Shim stock is available at auto parts stores.

5. Adjust throttle and Autolube pump cables.

Throttle Cable Adjustment

1. Refer to **Figure 23**. With engine idling, loosen locknut on top of carburetor.

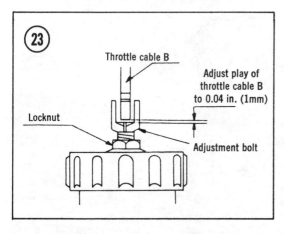

2. Turn the adjustment bolt to provide 0.04 in. (1.0mm) slack in throttle cable (B).

3. Tighten locknut.

4. Check this adjustment by pulling throttle cable (B). Engine speed should not increase until cable has been pulled up about 0.04 in. (1.0mm).

5. Refer to **Figure 24**. Loosen locknut, then turn adjuster to provide 0.02-0.04 in. (0.5-1.0mm) play.

6. Tighten locknut.

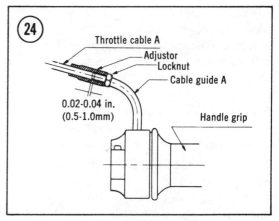

Autolube Cable Adjustment

1. Refer back to Figure 21. With engine not running, loosen locknut.

2. Close throttle fully.

3. Open throttle slowly until all slack in throttle cable is taken up. Hold throttle grip in this position during adjustment procedure.

4. Turn cable adjustment nut until mark on pulley aligns with guide pin.

5. Tighten locknut.

BATTERY SERVICE

Tune-up time is also battery service time. Complete battery service information is contained in Chapter Six. Briefly, the following items should be attended to regularly.

1. Test state of charge. Recharge if at half charge (1.220 specific gravity) or less.

2. Add distilled water if required.

3. Clean battery top.

4. Clean and tighten terminals.

OIL CHANGE

Probably the single most important maintenance item which contributes to long transmission life is that of regular oil changes. Oil becomes contaminated with products of combustion, condensation, and dirt. Some of these contaminants react with oil, forming acids which attack vital components, and thereby result in premature wear.

To change oil, first ride the bike until it is throughly warm. Place a flat pan under the engine, then remove the oil drain plug from the bottom of the engine and allow oil to drain. It may be helpful to rock the motorcycle from side to side and also forward and backward to get out as much oil as possible.

Replace the drain plug, then refill with fresh engine oil which meets API specification MS or SE. Maintain oil level between both marks on the dipstick.

CLUTCH ADJUSTMENT

Only routine clutch adjustment is discussed in this section. Refer to Chapter Four for details of major clutch service. Clutches on these models may be described as Type 1 (**Figure 25**) or Type 2 (**Figure 26**).

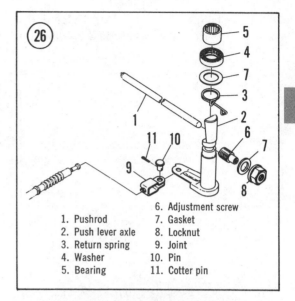

1. Pushrod
2. Push lever axle
3. Return spring
4. Washer
5. Bearing
6. Adjustment screw
7. Gasket
8. Locknut
9. Joint
10. Pin
11. Cotter pin

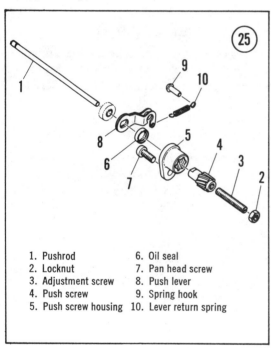

1. Pushrod
2. Locknut
3. Adjustment screw
4. Push screw
5. Push screw housing
6. Oil seal
7. Pan head screw
8. Push lever
9. Spring hook
10. Lever return spring

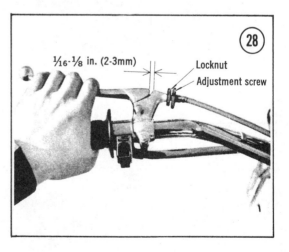

1/16-1/8 in. (2-3mm) Locknut Adjustment screw

Type 1

1. Refer to **Figure 27**. Loosen locknut.

2. Turn adjuster screw in until it seats lightly, then back it out ¼ turn.

3. Tighten locknut. Be sure that adjuster screw does not turn as nut is tightened.

4. Refer to **Figure 28**. Loosen locknut, then turn cable adjuster to obtain about 1/16-1/8 in. (2-3mm) cable slack at clutch lever.

5. Tighten cable adjuster locknut.

Type 2

1. Remove sprocket cover or clutch adjuster cover.

2. Loosen locknut.

3. Turn Phillips screw until lever (**Figure 29**) makes 10 degree angle with transmission main shaft centerline.

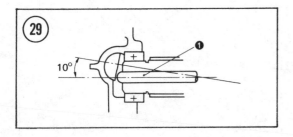

4. Tighten locknut.

5. Replace cover.

6. Refer back to Figure 28. Loosen locknut, then turn cable adjuster to obtain about 1/16-1/8 in. (2-3mm) cable slack at clutch lever.

ELECTRICAL EQUIPMENT

Check all electrical equipment for proper operation—lights, horn, starter, etc. Refer to Chapter Six for electrical system service.

DRIVE CHAIN

Clean, lubricate, and adjust the drive chain every 1,000 miles (1,500 kilometers) or more often as needed. Adjust drive chain tension to provide ¾-1 in. (20-25mm) up and down play in the center of the lower chain run. Both wheels should be on the ground and a rider in the saddle when this measurement is made. Be sure to adjust the rear brake after chain tension adjustment.

BRAKES

Adjust front and rear brakes every 1,000 miles (1,500 kilometers), or more often as needed. Remove wheels and check brake lining at 6,000-mile (9,000-kilometer) intervals. Check and service wheel bearings at the same time. See Chapter Seven for required procedures.

WHEELS AND TIRES

Check wheels for bent rims and loose or missing spokes. Complete wheel inspection and service procedures are detailed in Chapter Seven.

STEERING HEAD BEARINGS

Check steering head bearings for looseness or binding. *If any exists, find out and correct the cause immediately.* Complete service instructions are in Chapter Seven.

CHAPTER THREE

TROUBLESHOOTING

Diagnosing motorcycle ills is relatively simple if you use orderly procedures and keep a few basic principles in mind.

Never assume anything. Don't overlook the obvious. If you are riding along and the bike suddenly quits, check the easiest, most accessible problem spots first. Is there gasoline in the tank? Is the gas petcock in the ON or RESERVE position? Has the spark plug wire fallen off? Check the ignition switch. Sometimes the weight of keys on a key ring may turn the ignition off suddenly.

If nothing obvious turns up in a cursory check, look a little further. Learning to recognize and describe symptoms will make repairs easier for you or a mechanic at the shop. Describe problems accurately and fully. Saying that "it won't run" isn't the same as saying "it quit on the highway at high speed and wouldn't start", or that "it sat in my garage for three months and then wouldn't start".

Gather as many symptoms together as possible to aid in diagnosis. Note whether the engine lost power gradually or all at once, what color smoke (if any) came from the exhaust, and so on. Remember that the more complex a machine is, the easier it is to troubleshoot because symptoms point to specific problems.

You don't need fancy equipment or complicated test gear to determine whether repairs can be attempted at home. A few simple checks could save a large repair bill and time lost while the bike sits in a dealer's service department. On the other hand, be realistic and don't attempt repairs beyond your abilities. Service departments tend to charge heavily for putting together a disassembled engine that may have been abused. Some won't even take on such a job— so use common sense; don't get in over your head.

OPERATING REQUIREMENTS

An engine needs 3 basics to run properly: correct gas/air mixture, compression, and a spark at the right time. If one or more are missing, the engine won't run. The electrical system is the weakest link of the three. More problems result from electrical breakdowns than from any other source. Keep that in mind before you begin tampering with carburetor adjustments and the like.

If a bike has been sitting for any length of time and refuses to start, check the battery (if the machine is so equipped) for a charged condition first, and then look to the gasoline delivery system. This includes the tank, fuel petcocks, lines, and the carburetor. Rust may have formed in the tank, obstructing fuel flow. Gasoline deposits may have gummed up carburetor jets and air passages. Gasoline tends to lose its potency after standing for long periods. Condensation may contaminate it with water. Drain old gas and try starting with a fresh tankful.

Compression, or the lack of it, usually enters the picture only in the case of older machines. Worn or broken pistons, rings, and cylinder bores could prevent starting. Generally a gradual power loss and harder and harder starting will be readily apparent in this case.

STARTING DIFFICULTIES

Check gas flow first. Remove the gas cap and look into the tank. If gas is present, pull off a fuel line at the carburetor and see if gas flows freely. If none comes out, the fuel tap may be shut off, blocked by rust or foreign matter, or the fuel line may be stopped up or kinked. If the carburetor is getting usable fuel, turn to the electrical system next.

Check that the battery is charged by turning on the lights or by beeping the horn. Refer to your owner's manual for starting procedures with a dead battery. Have the battery recharged if necessary.

Pull off the spark plug cap, remove the spark plug, and reconnect the cap. Lay the plug against the cylinder head so its base makes a good connection, and turn the engine over with the kickstarter. A fat, blue spark should jump across the electrodes. If there is no spark, or a weak one, there is electrical system trouble. Check for a defective plug by replacing it with a known good one. Don't assume a plug is good just because it's new.

Once the plug has been cleared of guilt, but there's still no spark, start backtracking through the system. If the contact at the end of the spark plug wire can be exposed, it can be held about ⅛ inch from the head while the engine is turned over to check for a spark. Remember to hold the wire only by its insulation to avoid a nasty shock. If the plug wires are dirty, greasy, or wet, wrap a rag around them so you don't get shocked. If you do feel a shock or see sparks along the wire, clean or replace the wire and/or its connections.

If there's no spark at the plug wire, look for loose connections at the coil and battery. If all

seems in order here, check next for oily or dirty contact points. Clean points with electrical contact cleaner, or a strip of paper. On battery ignition models, with the ignition switch turned on, open and close the points manually with a screwdriver.

No spark at the points with this test indicates a failure in the ignition system. Refer to Chapter Six (*Electrical System*) for checkout procedures for the entire system and individual components. Refer to the same chapter for checking and setting ignition timing.

Note that spark plugs of the incorrect heat range (too cold) may cause hard starting. Set gap to specifications. If you have just ridden through a puddle or washed the bike and it won't start, dry off the plug and plug wire. Water may have entered the carburetor and fouled the fuel under these conditions, but a wet plug and wire are the more likely problem.

If a healthy spark occurs at the right time, and there is adequate gas flow to the carburetor, check the carburetor itself at this time. Make sure all jets and air passages are clean, check float level, and adjust if necessary. Shake the float to check for gasoline inside it, and replace or repair as indicated. Check that the carburetor is mounted snugly, and no air is leaking past the mounting flange. Check for a clogged air filter.

Compression may be checked in the field by turning the kickstarter by hand and noting that an adequate resistance is felt, or by removing the spark plug and placing a finger over the plug hole and feeling for pressure.

An accurate compression check gives a good idea of the condition of the basic working parts of the engine. To perform this test, you need a compression gauge. The motor should be warm.

1. Remove the plug from the cylinder to be tested and clean out any dirt or grease.

2. Insert the tip of the gauge into the hole, making sure it is seated correctly.

3. Open the throttle all the way.

4. Crank the engine several times and record the highest pressure reading on the gauge. Refer to Chapter Two (*Periodic Maintenance*) to interpret results.

POOR IDLING

Poor idling may be caused by incorrect carburetor adjustment, incorrect timing, or ignition system defects. Check the gas cap vent for an obstruction. Also check for loose carburetor mounting bolts or a poor carburetor flange gasket.

MISFIRING

Misfiring can be caused by a weak spark or dirty plugs. Check for fuel contamination. Run the machine at night or in a darkened garage to check for spark leaks along the plug wires and under the spark plug cap. If misfiring occurs only at certain throttle settings, refer to the carburetor chapter for the specific carburetor circuits involved. Misfiring under heavy load, as when climbing hills or accelerating, is usually caused by bad spark plugs.

FLAT SPOTS

If the engine seems to die momentarily when the throttle is opened and then recovers, check for a dirty main jet in the carburetor, water in the fuel, or an excessively lean mixture.

POWER LOSS

Poor condition of rings, pistons, or cylinders will cause a lack of power and speed. Ignition timing should be checked.

OVERHEATING

If the engine seems to run too hot all the time, be sure you are not idling it for long periods. Air-cooled engines are not designed to operate at a standstill for any length of time. Heavy stop and go traffic is hard on a motorcycle engine. Spark plugs of the wrong heat range can burn pistons. An excessively lean gas mixture may cause overheating. Check ignition timing. Don't ride in too high a gear. Broken or worn rings may permit compression gases to leak past them, heating heads and cylinders excessively. Check oil level and use the proper grade lubricants.

BACKFIRING

Check that the timing is not advanced too far. Check fuel for contamination.

ENGINE NOISES

Experience is needed to diagnose accurately in this area. Noises are hard to differentiate and harder yet to describe. Deep knocking noises usually mean main bearing failure. A slapping noise generally comes from loose pistons. A light knocking noise during acceleration may be a bad connecting rod bearing. Pinging, which sounds like marbles being shaken in a tin can, is caused by ignition advanced too far or gasoline with too low an octane rating. Pinging should be corrected immediately or damage to pistons will result. Compression leaks at the head/cylinder joint will sound like a rapid on and off squeal.

PISTON SEIZURE

Piston seizure is caused by incorrect piston clearances when fitted, fitting rings with improper end gap, too thin an oil being used, incorrect spark plug heat range, or incorrect ignition timing. Overheating from any cause may result in seizure.

EXCESSIVE VIBRATION

Excessive vibration may be caused by loose motor mounts, worn engine or transmission bearings, loose wheels, worn swinging arm bushings, a generally poor running engine, broken or cracked frame, or one that has been damaged in a collision. See also *Poor Handling*.

CLUTCH SLIP OR DRAG

Clutch slip may be due to worn plates, improper adjustment, or glazed plates. A dragging clutch could result from damaged or bent plates, improper adjustment, or even clutch spring pressure.

POOR HANDLING

Poor handling may be caused by improper tire pressures, a damaged frame or swinging arm, worn shocks or front forks, weak fork springs, a bent or broken steering stem, misaligned wheels, loose or missing spokes, worn tires, bent handlebars, worn wheel bearings, or dragging brakes.

3

BRAKE PROBLEMS

Sticking brakes may be caused by broken or weak return springs, improper cable or rod adjustment, or dry pivot and cam bushings. Grabbing brakes may be caused by greasy linings which must be replaced. Brake grab may also be due to out-of-round drums or linings which have broken loose from the brake shoes. Glazed linings will cause loss of stopping power.

LIGHTING PROBLEMS

Bulbs which continuously burn out may be caused by excessive vibration, loose connections that permit sudden current surges, poor battery connections, or installation of the wrong type bulb.

A dead battery or one which discharges quickly may be caused by a faulty generator or rectifier. Check for loose or corroded terminals. Shorted battery cells or broken terminals will keep a battery from charging. Low water level will decrease a battery's capacity. A battery left uncharged after installation will sulphate, rendering it useless.

A majority of light and horn or other electrical accessory problems are caused by loose or corroded ground connections. Check those first, and then substitute known good units for easier troubleshooting.

TROUBLESHOOTING GUIDE

The following quick reference guide (**Table 1**) summarizes part of the troubleshooting process. Use this table to outline possible problem areas, then refer to the specific chapter or section involved.

Table 1   TROUBLESHOOTING GUIDE

Item	Problem or Cause	Things to Check
Loss of power	Poor compression	Piston rings and cylinder Head gaskets Crankcase leaks
	Overheated engine	Lubricating oil supply Clogged cooling fins Ignition timing Slipping clutch Carbon in combustion chamber
	Improper mixture	Dirty air cleaner Restricted fuel flow Gas cap vent hole
	Miscellaneous	Dragging brakes Tight wheel bearings Defective chain Clogged exhaust system
Steering	Hard steering	Tire pressures Steering damper adjustment Steering stem head Steering head bearings

(continued)

Table 1   **TROUBLESHOOTING GUIDE**   (continued)

Item	Problem or Cause	Things to Check
Steering (continued)	Pulls to one side	Unbalanced shock absorbers Drive chain adjustment Front/rear wheel alignment Unbalanced tires Defective swing arm Defective steering head
	Shimmy	Drive chain adjustment Loose or missing spokes Deformed rims Worn wheel bearings Wheel balance
Gearshifting difficulties	Clutch	Adjustment Springs Friction plates Steel plates Oil quantity
	Transmission	Oil quantity Oil grade Return spring or pin Change lever or spring Drum position plate Change drum Change forks
Brakes	Poor brakes	Worn linings Brake adjustment Oil or water on brake linings Loose linkage or cables
	Noisy brakes	Worn or scratched lining Scratched brake drums Dirt in brakes
	Unadjustable brakes	Worn linings Worn drums Worn brake cams

3

CHAPTER FOUR

ENGINE, TRANSMISSION, AND CLUTCH

This chapter describes removal, disassembly, service, and reassembly of the engine, transmission, and clutch. The engine should be serviced without removing it from the chassis except for overhaul of the crankshaft assembly, transmission, or bearings. Operating principles of 2-stroke engines are also discussed in this chapter.

TWO-STROKE OPERATING PRINCIPLES

Figures 1 through 4 illustrate operating principles of piston port engines. During this discussion, assume that the crankshaft is rotating counterclockwise. In Figure 1, as the piston travels downward, scavenging port (A) between the crankcase and the cylinder is uncovered. Exhaust gases leave the cylinder through exhaust port (B), which is also opened by downward movement of the piston. A fresh fuel/air charge, which has previously been compressed slightly, travels from crankcase (C) to the cylinder through scavenging port (A) as the port opens. Since the incoming charge is under pressure, it rushes into the cylinder quickly and helps to expel exhaust gases from the previous cycle.

Figure 2 illustrates the next phase of the cycle. As the crankshaft continues to rotate, the piston moves upward, closing the exhaust and

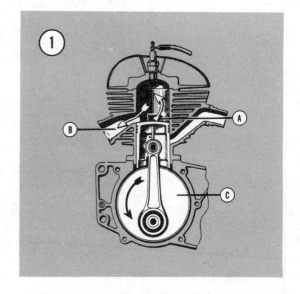

scavenging ports. As the piston continues upward, the air/fuel mixture in the cylinder is compressed. Notice also that a low pressure area is created in the crankcase at the same time. Further upward movement of the piston uncovers intake port (D). A fresh fuel/air charge is then drawn into the crankcase through the intake port because of the low pressure created by the upward piston movement.

The third phase is shown in Figure 3. As the piston approaches top dead center, the spark

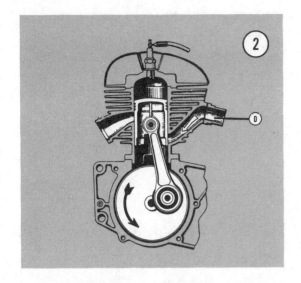

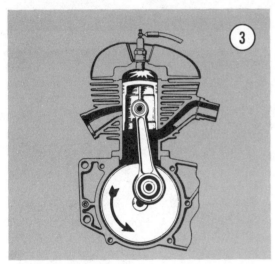

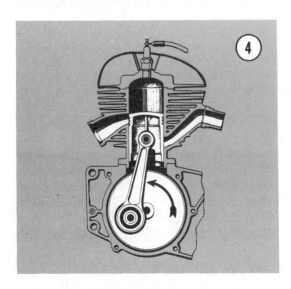

plug fires, igniting the compressed mixture. The piston is then driven downward by the expanding gases.

When the top of the piston uncovers the exhaust port, the fourth phase begins, as shown in Figure 4. The exhaust gases leave the cylinder through the exhaust port. As the piston continues downward, the intake port is closed and the mixture in the crankcase is compressed in preparation for the next cycle.

For best performance in 2-cycle engines, burned gases from one cycle must be completely expelled from the cylinder, and a maximum charge of fresh fuel/air mixture must be admitted into the cylinder in preparation for the next power stroke.

In conventional engines, if inlet port timing is increased, complete closure of the inlet port will be delayed, and the fuel/air mixture may tend to flow backward through the carburetor. Yamaha's reed valve induction system functions as a one-way valve which prevents reverse fuel mixture flow. The following paragraphs discuss operation of the reed valve.

Figure 5 illustrates system operation as the piston begins to move upward from bottom dead center. The piston begins to close the exhaust port. Fuel/air mixture entering the cylinder forces burned gases out through the exhaust port. As the piston continues upward, crankcase pressure becomes negative, and the holes in the piston skirt uncover the inlet port. Fuel/air mixture then begins to flow into the crankcase through the reed valve and the holes in the piston skirt.

Figure 6 shows the piston as it nears firing position. All cylinder ports are closed, and the combustion chamber is now completely sealed, so the entrapped fuel/air mixture is compressed. The piston skirt has cleared the intake port, so fresh fuel/air mixture continues to be drawn into the crankcase through the open reed valve and intake port.

The spark plug fires and ignites the mixture, driving the piston downward (**Figure 7**). As the piston moves downward, the fuel/air mixture in the crankcase starts to become compressed. Although the holes in the piston skirt open the intake port, the closed reed valve prevents the

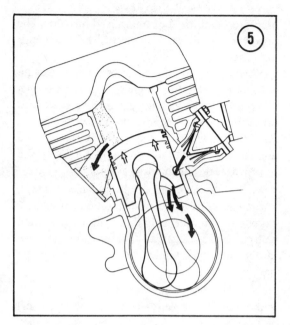

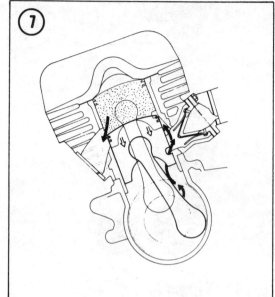

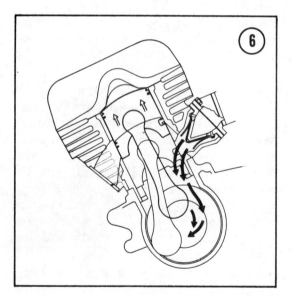

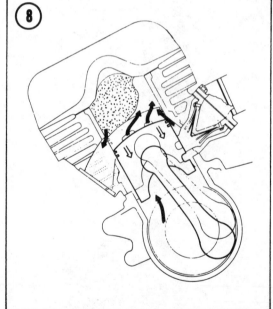

mixture from backing up through the carburetor.

Figure 8 illustrates system operation after the piston has cleared the exhaust port. The mixture in the crankcase has been further compressed. The burned exhaust gases leave the cylinder through the exhaust port. The piston opens the transfer ports shortly after the exhaust port opens. Four streams of fresh fuel/air mixture rush into the cylinder through the transfer ports to help expel residual gases.

Figure 9 illustrates operation of the seventh port. As the piston lowers to the position illustrated, inertia of the exhaust gases leaving the cylinder, plus the incoming fuel/air mixture, causes the reed valve to open, and draw more fuel/air mixture directly into the cylinder. This mixture, which enters through the seventh port, completely bypasses the crankcase.

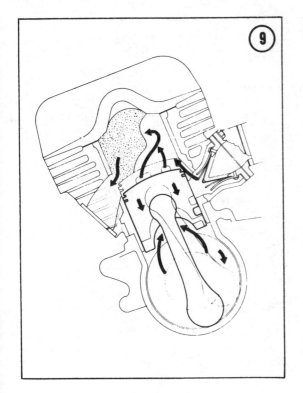

ENGINE LUBRICATION

It can be seen from the foregoing discussion that the engine cannot receive its lubrication from an oil supply in the crankcase. Oil splash in the crankcase would be carried into the cylinder with the fuel/air charge, resulting in high oil consumption and spark plug fouling. Yamaha 2-stroke engines use one of 2 methods for engine lubrication.

Fuel and Oil Mixture

Some competition models are lubricated by oil premixed with fuel. Sufficient oil is added to the fuel to provide adequate lubrication for the engine under the high speed and load conditions found in competition. Under low speed and load conditions, however, the engine receives more oil than is necessary, resulting in possible plug fouling. In addition, oil starvation can occur in prolonged periods during which the engine turns at high speeds with the throttle closed, as when descending a long hill. These situations do not occur during competition, but could cause problems for machines intended for street use.

Autolube System

To overcome objections to the oil/fuel mixture lubrication method, Yamaha developed its Autolube system. This system is used on most models. A separate engine driven oil pump (**Figure 10**) supplies oil to the engine induction tract. Oil output from the pump is controlled not only by engine speed, but also by throttle position, which is closely related to engine load. The engine is thereby supplied with the proper amount of oil under all operating conditions.

Air will enter the Autolube pump whenever the oil supply has run out, or the pump is removed or disconnected. Any air entrapped in the pump or oil lines will result in irregular and inadequate engine lubrication. After such an occurrence, the pump must be bled.

Bleeding the Autolube System

To bleed the pump, first remove the bleeder screw shown in **Figure 11**, then rotate the starter plate in the direction of the arrow. Continue to turn the starter plate until no more oil comes out, then replace the bleeder screw. Entrapped air will be bled out more quickly if the throttle is held fully open as the starter plate is rotated.

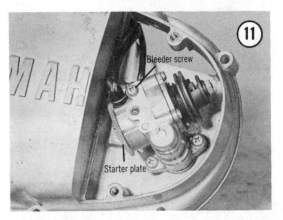

Refer to Chapter Two for details of Autolube pump adjustment.

PREPARATION FOR ENGINE DISASSEMBLY

1. Thoroughly clean the engine exterior of dirt, oil, and foreign material, using one of the cleaners formulated for the purpose.

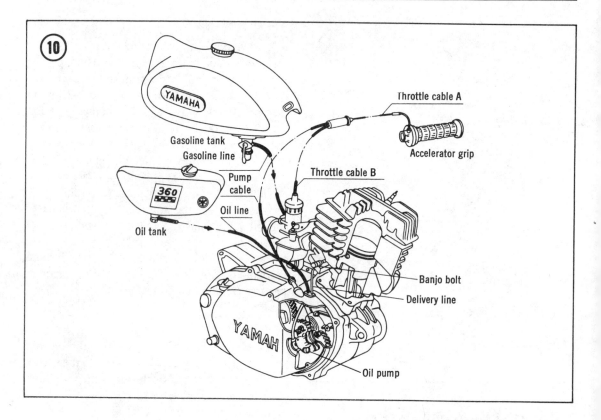

2. Be sure that you have the proper tools for the job. See *Tools* in Chapter One.

3. As you remove parts from the engine, clean them and place them in trays in the order of their disassembly. Doing so will make assembly faster and easier, and will ensure correct installation of all engine parts. Keep all related parts together.

4. Note that the disassembly procedures vary slightly between the different models. Be sure to read all steps carefully and follow those which apply to your engine.

ENGINE REMOVAL/INSTALLATION

This procedure is similar for all models. The following steps are set forth as a guide. Special instructions for individual models are also noted in the procedures.

1. Start the engine and run it a few minutes to warm the transmission oil. Stop the engine and immediately drain the transmission oil. The drain plug is located on the bottom of the transmission case, as shown in **Figure 12**.

2. Remove the muffler or expansion chamber. On models with through-frame mufflers, detach all retaining hardware, then slide the muffler forward for removal. On models so equipped, unhook both springs at the cylinder, then remove both muffler retaining bolts. On other models, remove the exhaust pipe retaining bolts at the cylinder and those which attach the muffler.

3. Remove the gearshift pedal. It is necessary to completely remove its retaining bolt before the pedal can be pulled from its shaft.

4. Remove the left crankcase cover.

5. Disconnect all wiring from the engine. Do not forget to disconnect the wire at the neutral switch on models so equipped.

6. Remove the master link, then the drive chain. It may be necessary to rotate the rear wheel to position the master link for convenient removal. When installing the chain, be sure to position the master link clip as shown in **Figure 13**.

> NOTE: *If the engine sprocket is to be removed, loosen its retaining nut at this time. With the rear brake applied, the drive chain will prevent the sprocket from turning as the nut is loosened.*

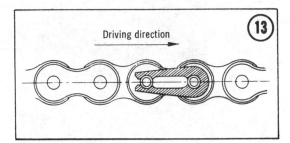

Driving direction ⑬

7. Remove the Autolube pump cover (if so equipped), then unwind the cable from the pump pulley and disconnect it. Completely remove the cable adjuster from the engine case.

> NOTE: *After the cable installation, operate the throttle to ensure that the cable is wound around the pulley properly.*

8. Disconnect the tachometer drive cable at the lower end, where it screws into the engine case.

9. Disconnect the clamps which secure the rubber boot between the carburetor and air cleaner, then remove the rubber boot.

10. Disconnect the oil line at the tank. Be sure to plug the hole to prevent oil from flowing out.

11. Free the throttle cable from the carburetor. Unscrew the carburetor cap, then pull the slide out to free the cable. Anchor the slide and attached throttle cable out of the way.

CAUTION
When installing the slide, be sure that the cutaway on the lower end of the slide is toward the air cleaner.

12. Disconnect the fuel line at the fuel petcock. Be sure that the petcock is closed.

13. Disconnect the clutch cable if it is still attached. On most models, it will have been removed with the left crankcase cover.

14. Remove the spark plug cap.

15. Remove all engine mount bolts.

16. Straddle the machine and remove the engine from the frame.

17. Reverse the removal procedure to install the engine. Be sure to check the following items before starting the engine:

   a. Oil supply

   b. Autolube pump attachment

   c. Clutch adjustment

   d. Oil pump and throttle cables

   e. Drive chain adjustment

   f. Engine mounting bolts

   g. Ignition timing

   h. Transmission oil level (**Table 1**)

Table 1 OIL QUANTITY

Engine Size	Ounces	Milliliter
250 (to 1974)	34	1,000
250 (1974 on)	41	1,200
360 (1974 on)	41	1,200
400	34	1,000

CYLINDER AND CYLINDER HEAD

Cylinder Head Removal/Installation

With the engine cold, loosen each cylinder head nut a little bit at a time, in crisscross order, until all are loose. Then remove all nuts. Lift the cylinder head from the cylinder (**Figure 14**). It may be necessary to tap the head lightly with a rubber mallet to free it; if so, take care not to break any cooling fins.

Upon installation, always use a new cylinder head gasket. Torque cylinder head nuts in crisscross order to 14.5 ft.-lb. (2.0 mkg) on all models except those with 8mm and 10mm nuts. Torque 10mm nuts to 25.3 ft.-lb. (3.5 mkg) first, then torque 8mm nuts to 14.5 ft.-lb. (2.0 mkg).

Removing Carbon Deposits

Carbon deposits in the combustion chamber cause increased compression ratio and may lead to preignition, overheating, and excessive fuel consumption. To remove these deposits, scrape them off with the rounded end of a hacksaw blade, as shown in **Figure 15**. Be careful not to damage the gasket surface.

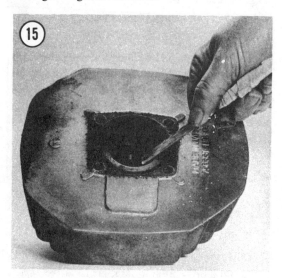

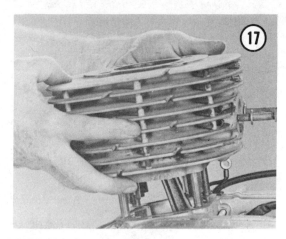

Cylinder Removal

With the cylinder head and oil pump delivery tube (**Figure 16**) removed, tap the cylinder around the exhaust port with a plastic mallet, then pull it away from the crankcase (**Figure 17**). Stuff a clean rag into the crankcase opening to prevent entry of any foreign material.

Cylinders on some models are retained by additional nuts. Loosen these nuts in a criss-cross order ¼ turn at a time until all are loose, then remove them before removing the cylinder.

Checking the Cylinder

Measure cylinder wall wear at locations (a), (b), (c), and (d) with a cylinder gauge or inside micrometer, as shown in **Figure 18**. Position the instrument parallel, and then at right angles to the crankshaft at each depth. If the difference between any measurements exceeds 0.0018 in. (0.05mm), rebore and hone the cylinder to the next oversize, or replace the cylinder. Pistons are available in oversizes of 0.01 in. (0.25mm) and 0.02 in. (0.50mm). After boring and honing, the difference between maximum and minimum diameters must not be greater than 0.0004 in. (0.01mm).

Removing Carbon Deposits

Scrape carbon deposits from around the cylinder exhaust port, as shown in **Figure 19**. The rounded end of a hacksaw blade is a suitable tool for carbon removal.

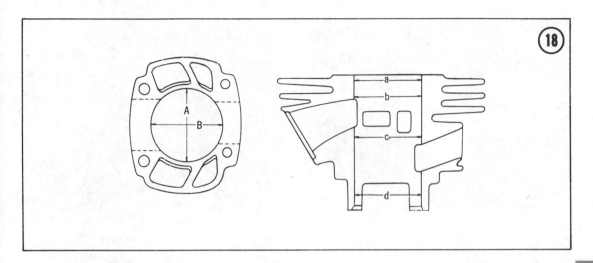

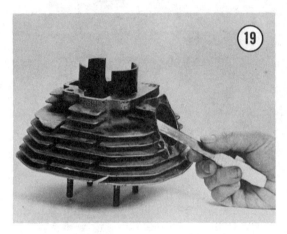

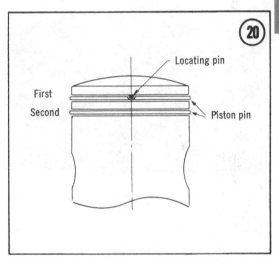

Cylinder Installation

Be sure that each piston ring end gap is aligned with its locating pin in the ring groove (**Figure 20**). Lubricate the piston and cylinder, then insert the piston into the lower end of the cylinder. It will be necessary to compress each piston ring as it goes into the cylinder. Always use a new cylinder base gasket upon reassembly, and be sure that all traces of old gasket are removed.

On models with cylinder retaining nuts, tighten them in crisscross order, in progressive stages, to 25-29 ft.-lb. (3.5-4.0 mkg).

> ### CAUTION
> *During base gasket installation, make sure the gasket is placed correctly on the crankcase. Check that the gasket matches the irregularly shaped transfer port channels.*

PISTON, PIN, AND RINGS

Remove the clip at each end of the piston pin with needle nose pliers (**Figure 21**). Press out the piston pin (**Figure 22**). It may be helpful to first heat the piston by wrapping it in rags soaked in hot water. In particularly stubborn cases, it is possible to make a simple puller from a length of threaded rod and a few pieces of scrap material (**Figure 23**).

After long service, a ridge may build up around the piston pin clip groove, which makes piston pin removal difficult. In such cases, do not drive the piston pin out by hammering it. Protect the crankcase opening with rags, then carefully chamfer the raised outer groove edge with a knife to scrape away this ridge. The pin should then slide out easily.

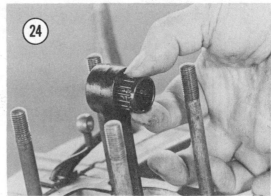

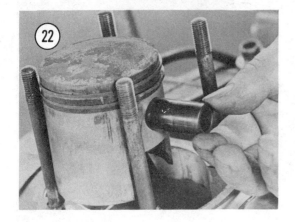

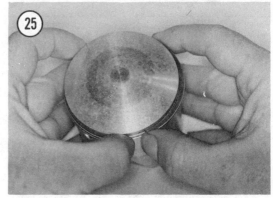

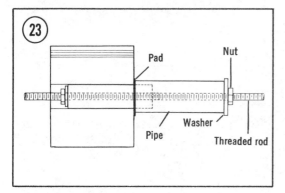

Measure each ring for wear as shown in **Figure 26**. Insert the ring 0.2 in. (5mm) into the cylinder, then measure ring gap with a feeler gauge. To ensure that the ring is squarely in the cylinder, push it into position with the head of the piston (**Figure 27**). If gap is not as specified in **Table 2**, replace the piston rings.

Remove the upper bearing from the connecting rod (**Figure 24**).

Piston Rings

Remove the piston rings by spreading the top ring with a thumb on each end, as shown in **Figure 25**. Then remove the ring from the top of the piston. Repeat this procedure for the remaining ring. Some models are equipped with only one ring.

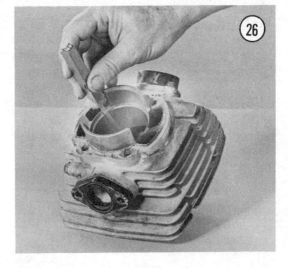

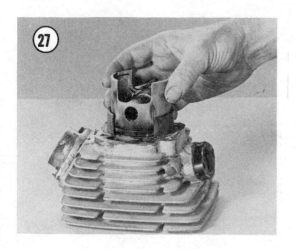

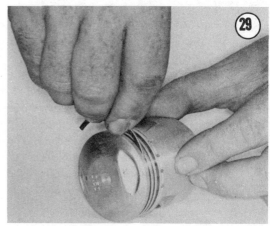

Table 2   PISTON RING GAP

| Engine Size | End Gap | |
	Inch	Millimeter
250	0.008-0.016	0.20-0.40
250 (GYT)	0.016-0.020	0.40-0.50
360	0.012-0.020	0.30-0.50
360 (GYT)	0.016-0.020	0.40-0.50
400	0.016-0.020	0.40-0.50
Keystone rings	0.012-0.020	0.30-0.50

To check fit of the piston ring in its groove, slip the outer surface of the ring into the groove next to the locating pin, then roll the ring completely around the piston (**Figure 30**). If any binding occurs, determine and correct the cause before proceeding. Side clearance tolerances are specified in **Table 3**.

Scrape carbon deposits from the head of the piston (**Figure 28**). Then clean all carbon and gum from the piston ring grooves (**Figure 29**) using a broken piston ring, or a ring groove cleaning tool. Any deposits left in the grooves will cause the rings to stick, leading to gas blow-by and loss of power.

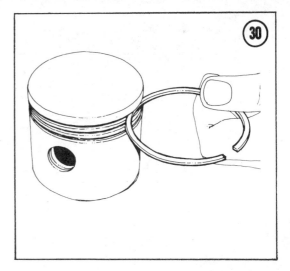

Table 3   PISTON RING SIDE CLEARANCE

| Engine Size | Side Clearance | |
	Inch	Millimeter
250	0.0012-0.0028	0.03-0.07
250 (GYT)	0.0016-0.0032	0.04-0.08
360	0.0012-0.0028	0.03-0.07
400	0.0012-0.0028	0.03-0.07

When replacing rings, install the lower one first. Be sure that any printing on the ring is toward the top of the piston. Spread the rings carefully with your theumbs, just enough to slip them over the pistons. Align end gaps with the locating pin in each ring groove.

Some machines are equipped with Keystone pistons and rings. Keystone and conventional rings are compared in **Figures 31 and 32**. The design of the Keystone ring uses combustion gas pressure to force the ring outward against the cylinder wall (**Figure 33**).

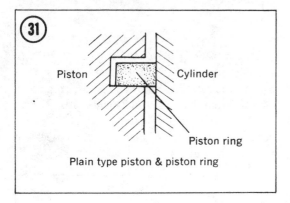

Plain type piston & piston ring

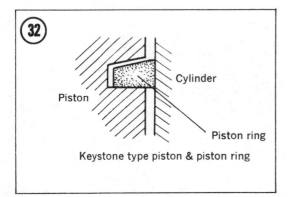

Keystone type piston & piston ring

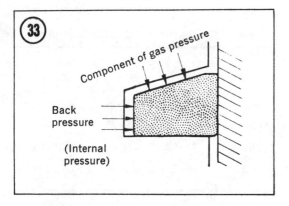

An important advantage of the Keystone ring is illustrated in **Figure 34**. As the piston moves up and down, the piston ring tends to move inward and outward, thus varying ring land clearance. This varying clearance tends to prevent the ring from sticking in its groove.

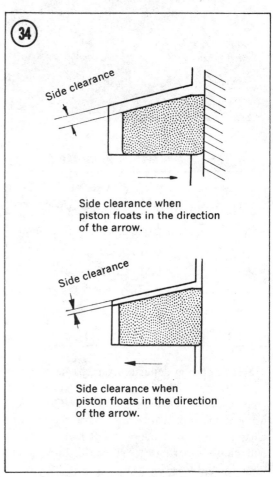

Side clearance when piston floats in the direction of the arrow.

Side clearance when piston floats in the direction of the arrow.

The outer surface of the Keystone ring is Teflon coated. This Teflon coating aids ring seating. Also, the coating tends to follow microscopic irregularities in the cylinder, thereby reducing blow-by.

Keystone rings can be identified by their shape; the top and bottom edges are not parallel. Keystone rings are not interchangeable with the conventional type, and must be used with Keystone pistons. Keystone pistons may be identified by the "K" stamped on the crown after the piston size. Keystone rings are handled in the same manner as conventional rings.

Piston Reconditioning

A piston exhibiting signs of seizure will result in noise, loss of power, and damage to the cylinder wall. If such a piston is reused without correction, another seizure will develop. To correct this condition, lightly smooth the affected area with No. 400 emery paper or a fine oilstone (**Figure 35**).

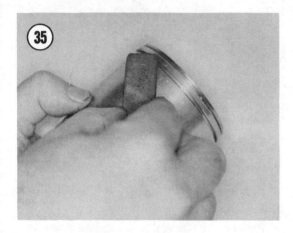

Replace the piston if the seizure marks cannot be removed with absolute minimal polishing. If in any doubt, replace the piston.

Carefully examine the entire piston surface. Check for cracks, partially melted piston crown, score marks, broken or deformed ring grooves, or any other damage that might interfere with correct piston performance. Replace the piston if any of these defects are noticed.

Checking and Correcting
Piston Clearance

Piston clearance is the difference between maximum piston diameter and minimum cylinder diameter. Measure outside diameter of the piston skirt (**Figure 36**) at right angles to the piston pin. The measurement should be made 0.2 in. (5mm) from the bottom of the piston. Proper piston clearances are listed in **Table 4**. Any clearance greater than 0.004 in. (0.10mm) will result in noise, in which case necessary repairs should be made.

Piston Installation

Install the piston with the arrow mark (**Figure 37**) pointing toward the front of the

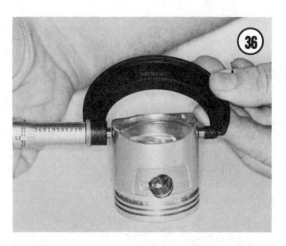

Table 4   PISTON CLEARANCE

Engine Size	Inch	Millimeter
250 (Enduro)	0.0016-0.0018	0.040-0.045
250 (MX and YZ)	0.0016-0.0020	0.040-0.050
RT-1, RT1-B	0.0022-0.0024	0.055-0.060
RT1-MX, RT1B-MX	0.0022-0.0024	0.055-0.060
MX 360	0.0022-0.0024	0.055-0.060
DT 360, MX 360 A	0.0016-0.0018	0.040-0.045
400	0.0020-0.0024	0.050-0.060

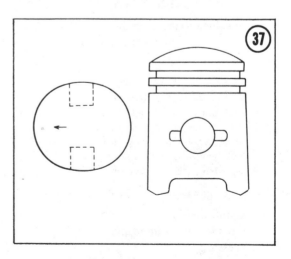

machine. This step is vital because the hole for the piston pin is offset slightly to prevent piston slap.

Piston Pin

The piston pin should fit snugly in its bore in the piston, so that it drags slightly as you turn it. If the piston pin is loose, replace the pin and/or the piston. If the pin shows step wear in the center, replace the needle bearing in the upper end of the connecting rod as well as the piston pin. Check the small end of the connecting rod for wear by assembling the piston pin and upper end bearing (**Figure 38**).

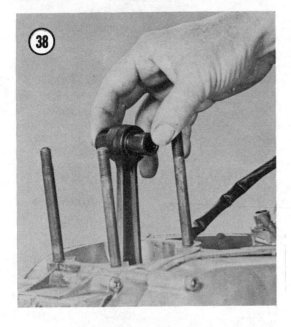

REED VALVE

Reed valve service is similar for all models so equipped. Pay particular attention to the instructions regarding handling of the assembly.

CAUTION
The reed valve is a precision component, and it must be handled with great care. Store the assembly in a clean, dry place, and do not expose it to sunlight. Take special care not to touch its working parts with your fingers.

Figure 39 illustrates reed valve construction.

   a. Stainless steel reeds, which open and close the inlet port in response to crankcase pressure changes

   b. Valve case

   c. Gasket

   d. Valve stop

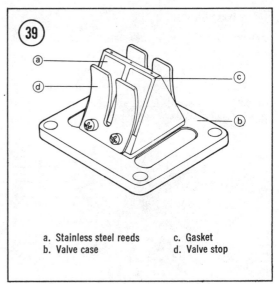

a. Stainless steel reeds   c. Gasket
b. Valve case   d. Valve stop

Removal/Installation

1. Remove carburetor.

2. Remove valve assembly.

3. Reverse the removal procedure to install the reed valve assembly.

Maintenance

Reed valve maintenance is limited to inspection of components and tightening of loose screws. Check for cracks or breakage. Be sure that the bond between the gasket and valve case is not broken. Tighten the screws to 4 ft.-lb. (8.0 cmkg). Replace the entire assembly if any component is defective.

COMPRESSION RELEASE

Some models are equipped with a compression release (**Figure 40**). When this device operates, it reduces engine compression to make starting easier. On earlier models, it is operated by a lever on the handlebar. On newer models, it is operated by the kickstarter (**Figure 41**).

To function properly, this device must be adjusted to provide full lever travel. Refer to **Figure 42**. When the compression release is in the *release* (engine starting) position, the end of the lever must come to within 0.020 in. (0.5mm) of the back plate, but it must not touch. If adjustment is necessary, follow the cable back to the cable adjuster, loosen the

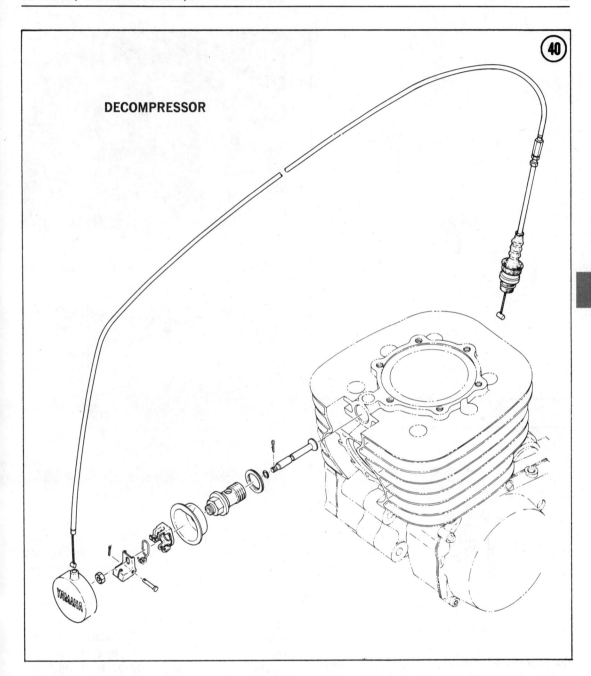

adjuster locknut, then turn the adjuster as required until correct lever clearance is achieved. Be sure to tighten the locknut and recheck lever clearance.

MAGNETO

Removal and installation only of this item is discussed in this chapter. Refer to Chapter Six for troubleshooting, or Chapter Two for routine service. Magneto removal and installation is generally similar for all models.

CAUTION
Do not attempt to remove the flywheel unless a suitable puller is available.

1. Remove flywheel retaining nut, flat washer, and lockwasher. A flywheel retaining tool is available or can be made locally, to hold the flywheel while its retaining nut is loosened. If

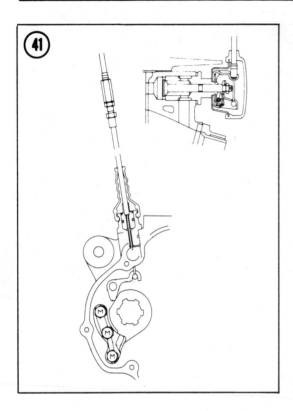

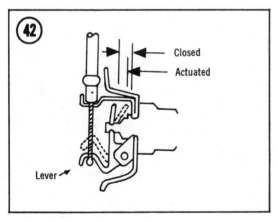

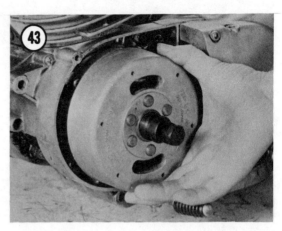

4. Remove the stator plate (**Figure 44**) after taking out its retaining screws.

5. Remove the Woodruff key from the crankshaft. To prevent this key from becoming lost, place it on one of the magnets inside the flywheel.

Reverse the foregoing procedure to install the magneto. Apply a very thin coating of distributor cam lubricant to the breaker cam inside the flywheel (**Figure 45**) before installation. Be sure that the Woodruff key is in place. Torque the flywheel retaining nut to 25-29 ft.-lb. (3.5-4.0 mkg) upon installation.

CAUTION
Before installing the flywheel, be sure that no particles adhere to the magnets.

ENGINE SPROCKET

Removal

1. Use a blunted chisel to straighten the tab on the lockwasher.

this tool is not available, a strap wrench works well. Another method is to feed a rolled-up rag between the primary reduction gears on the other side of the engine to prevent the engine from turning.

2. Screw a flywheel puller (left-hand thread) to its full depth into the flywheel center hole. Be sure that the puller screw is backed out fully before attaching the puller.

3. Turn the puller screw clockwise to remove the flywheel (**Figure 43**).

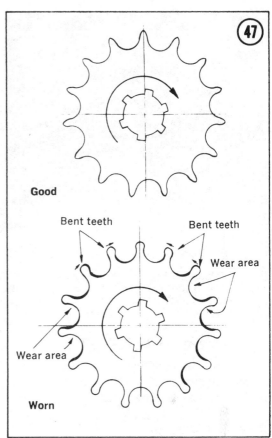

2. Remove retaining nut, then pull off the sprocket (**Figure 46**).

3. Using a pair of pliers, remove the sprocket spacer.

Inspection

Inspect sprocket teeth for wear. Excessive wear results in shortened drive chain life. Replace the sprocket if it is worn. **Figure 47** compares worn and serviceable sprockets.

Installation

Reverse the removal procedure to install the sprocket. Be sure to apply grease to the oil seal lip. Do not forget to bend up one edge of the lockwasher.

RIGHT CRANKCASE COVER

It is necessary to remove the right crankcase cover to gain access to the primary reduction gears, clutch, shifter, and kickstarter. It is not necessary to remove the Autolube pump to remove the cover.

Removal

NOTE: *There is a small quantity of oil under the cover. Place a suitable drain pan underneath before removing the cover. Also, be sure to check and replenish the transmission oil upon installation.*

1. Remove pinch bolt from kickstarter lever, then pull kickstarter lever from its shaft.
2. Remove oil delivery line at cylinder. See **Figure 48**.
3. Remove all cover retaining screws.
4. Rap cover with a rubber mallet if necessary, then pull it from engine.

Installation

Reverse the removal procedure to install the cover. Always install a new cover gasket. Replace the kickstarter oil seal if it leaks, or if its condition is doubtful.

AUTOLUBE PUMP

Removal and installation of the Autolube pump is discussed in this section. Refer to Chapter Two for details of pump adjustment.

Removal/Installation

1. Remove retaining nut and drive gear. See **Figure 49**.

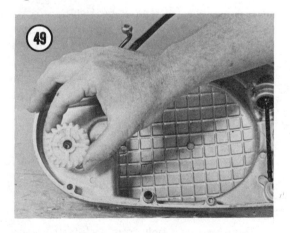

2. Pull out drive pin and washer (**Figure 50**).
3. Remove retainer clip (**Figure 51**).
4. Remove pump retainer screws (**Figure 52**).
5. Reverse Steps 1 through 4 to install the pump. Upon installation, always bleed the pump and adjust it.

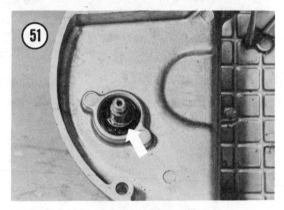

Air enters the pump whenever it has been disconnected or the oil supply has run out. After such an occurrence, the pump must be bled. Refer to **Figure 53**. Remove bleeder screw (A), then turn starter plate (B) in the direction of the arrow marked on it until no more air emerges from the bleeder screw hole. Entrapped air will be bled out more quickly if the throttle is held fully open during the bleeding procedure. Install the bleeder screw after all air is bled out.

CLUTCH

All models are equipped with wet multidisc clutches. Service on all clutches is similar; differences are pointed out where they exist. **Figures 54 and 55** are exploded views of typical clutches on these models. Refer to the applicable illustration during clutch service.

> NOTE: *When disassembling clutch, pay particular attention to the way that all small parts, such as spacers and thrust washers, are installed.*

1. Remove screws and springs (**Figure 56**).

2. Remove pressure plate (**Figure 57**).

3. Remove clutch hub retaining nut and lockwasher (**Figure 58**).

An easy way to fabricate a clutch holder is to weld a short handle to a discarded clutch plate. Another way to hold the clutch is to loop a fan belt of suitable length around the clutch, then secure its other end to the motorcycle frame.

4. Remove pushrod (**Figure 59**). There is a small steel ball behind this pushrod. Tip the engine to the right to remove it, or use a small magnet. Pull out long pushrod, if necessary, from left side of engine.

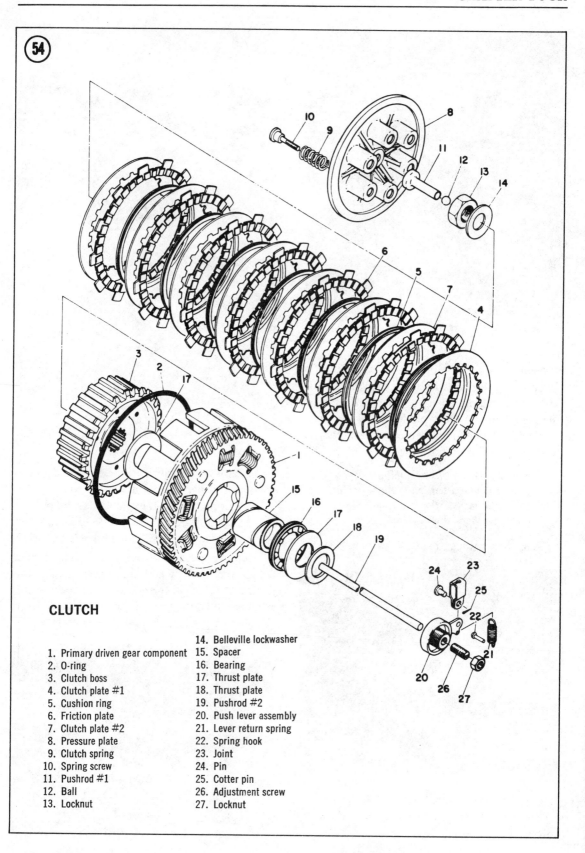

CLUTCH

1. Primary driven gear component
2. O-ring
3. Clutch boss
4. Clutch plate #1
5. Cushion ring
6. Friction plate
7. Clutch plate #2
8. Pressure plate
9. Clutch spring
10. Spring screw
11. Pushrod #1
12. Ball
13. Locknut
14. Belleville lockwasher
15. Spacer
16. Bearing
17. Thrust plate
18. Thrust plate
19. Pushrod #2
20. Push lever assembly
21. Lever return spring
22. Spring hook
23. Joint
24. Pin
25. Cotter pin
26. Adjustment screw
27. Locknut

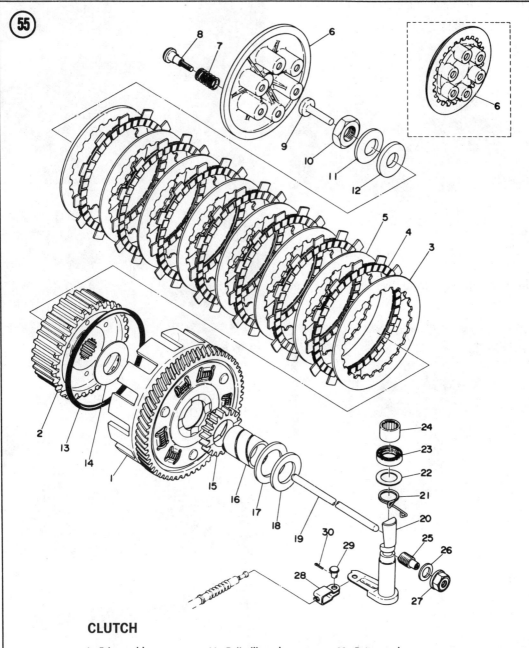

CLUTCH

1. Primary driven gear	11. Belleville spring	21. Return spring
2. Clutch boss	12. Spring washer	22. Washer
3. Clutch plate	13. O-ring	23. Oil seal
4. Friction plate	14. Thrust plate	24. Bearing
5. Clutch plate	15. Kick pinion gear	25. Adjusting screw
6. Pressure plate	16. Spacer	26. Gasket
7. Clutch spring	17. Thrust plate	27. Adjusting nut
8. Spring screw	18. Thrust plate	28. Joint
9. Pushrod	19. Pushrod	29. Pin
10. Locknut	20. Push lever axle	30. Cotter pin

5. Pull out all metal plates, fiber plates, and rubber rings (**Figure 60**).

6. Slide clutch hub from transmission input shaft (**Figure 61**).

7. Remove thrust washer (**Figure 62**).

8. Remove clutch housing (**Figure 63**).

9. Remove spacer (**Figure 64**) if it did not come off with clutch housing.

10. Remove flat thrust bearing and its associated washer (**Figure 65**).

11. If it is necessary to remove the spacer next to the transmission bearing, it is first necessary to remove the kickstarter idler gear (**Figure 66**).

Clutch Inspection

Measure free length of each clutch spring (**Figure 67**). If any spring is shorted by 0.04 in. (1.0mm) than the standard length specified in **Table 5**, replace all springs as a set.

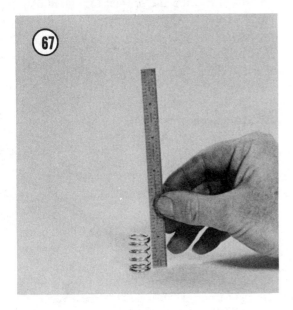

Measure thickness of each friction disc at several places (**Figure 68**). For all models, a new plate is 0.118 in. (3.0mm) thick. Replace any disc that is worn unevenly, or is less than 0.012 in. (0.30mm) thick.

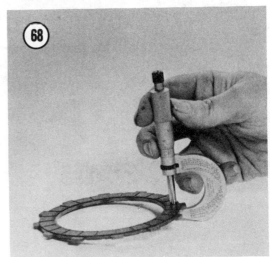

Check each metal plate for warpage by placing it on a surface plate. Then try to insert a 0.004 in. (0.10mm) feeler between the clutch plate and surface plate, from both the outside and inside. If the feeler slips between them, replace the clutch plate.

On some models, there is a rubber ring between the clutch housing and primary driven gear. This ring reduces gear noise at low engine speeds. Be sure that it is in good condition.

Be sure that the slots in the clutch hub and clutch housing are in good condition (**Figure 69**). If deep notches exist, they can hinder clutch disengagement.

Table 5   CLUTCH SPRING LENGTH

Model	Inch	Millimeter
DT2, Series	1.433	36.4
DT2, DT3	1.417	36.0
DT250	1.240	31.5
MX250	1.417	36.0
YZ250	1.279	32.5
RT1	1.433	36.4
RT2, RT2-MX, RT3	1.228	31.2
MX360	1.417	36.0
DT360	1.240	31.5
YZ360	1.279	32.5
400	1.626	41.3

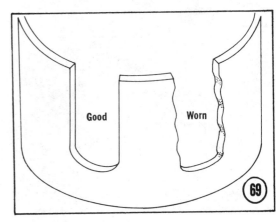

Good   Worn

Insert the primary gear spacer into the clutch housing bearing (**Figure 70**), then check for radial play. If play is excessive, replace the spacer. Allowable clearance is 0.004-0.0017 in. (0.01-0.048mm). Replace the spacer if it is scratched.

Check the gear teeth on the clutch housing for burrs, nicks, or other damage. Smooth any such defects with an oilstone. If the oilstone does not smooth out the damage, replace the clutch housing.

Remove all oil from the primary gear spacer and transmission main shaft. Then slide the spacer over the shaft (**Figure 71**) and measure clearance between them. Replace the spacer if radial clearance is not 0.008-0.0024 in. (0.020-0.062mm), or if the spacer exhibits step wear.

Remove the pushrod and check it for straightness by rolling it on a surface known to be flat. If the rod is bent, straighten or replace it.

Clutch Installation

1. Be sure that all thrust washers, plates, and bearings are in proper position.

2. Make sure both kick pinion gear protruding dogs engage the 2 squared-off slots in the back of the primary driven gear. Take care; there are also 2 rounded slots that the dogs could accidentally engage.

3. After installing the primary driven gear spacer, slide on the thrust bearing and washer, then carefully slide on the clutch housing. Take care; pulling the clutch housing out after it has been installed could easily dislodge the thrust washers or bearing and prevent the clutch housing from sliding in completely.

4. Slide in alternate metal and fiber plates. If your machine has rubber cushions, install one over the clutch hub after each metal plate. The open end faces out. Make sure they are not twisted. These cushions help separate the plates during disengagement. They are helpful, but not required for clutch operation.

NOTE: *If your model has an extra thick metal clutch plate, install this first onto the clutch hub, before any other plate.*

5. Install the long pushrod, ball bearing, and short pushrod into the transmission shaft hole.

6. Add the pressure plate, springs, and spring retaining screws. Tighten the spring retaining screws just until slightly snug. Excessive torque can snap the screws, which will require clutch hub replacement.

PRIMARY DRIVE GEAR

To remove the primary drive gear, feed a rolled-up rag between the primary drive and primary driven gears to lock them. Consider the direction the gears tend to turn as you loosen the locknut, then pull the gear from the crankshaft (**Figure 72**). If the gear does not come off easily, pry it off with a pair of heavy screwdrivers.

CAUTION
Always place rags or wood blocks between case and pry tools to prevent gasket surface damage.

After primary drive gear removal, an O-ring will be visible in a groove on the crankshaft. Make sure this O-ring is installed before primary drive gear installation. Failure to install it will result in fouled plugs and visible exhaust smoke because of transmission oil seeping past where the O-ring should be sealing. Replace this seal if it is flattened or nicked.

Always lubricate the crankshaft seal lips so the primary drive gear will slide through without tearing this seal.

KICKSTARTER

There are 3 basic types of kickstarter mechanisms on Yamaha models covered by this book. **Figures 73 through 75** are exploded views of each mechanism. Refer to the applicable illustration during disassembly, service, and reassembly.

Removal

Kickstarter removal is generally similar for all models.

1. Unhook kickstarter spring (**Figure 76**). Be careful; this spring is under considerable tension.

2. Rotate kickstarter shaft about 45 degrees counterclockwise to free it from the ratchet wheel guide, then pull it straight out (**Figure 77**).

3. On some models, there is a shim between the crankcase and kickstarter shaft. Be careful not to lose it.

4. Remove the snap ring and thrust washer, then pull the kickstarter idler gear from its shaft (**Figure 78**).

4

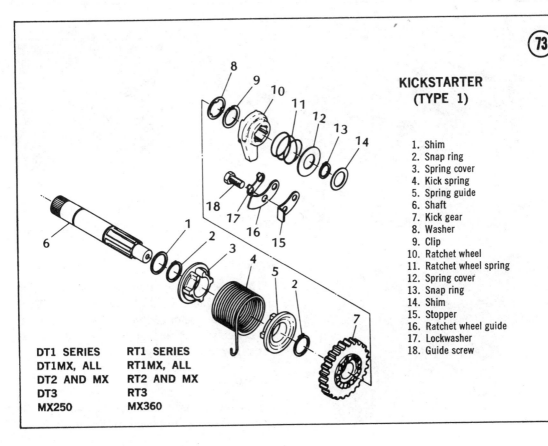

KICKSTARTER (TYPE 1)

1. Shim
2. Snap ring
3. Spring cover
4. Kick spring
5. Spring guide
6. Shaft
7. Kick gear
8. Washer
9. Clip
10. Ratchet wheel
11. Ratchet wheel spring
12. Spring cover
13. Snap ring
14. Shim
15. Stopper
16. Ratchet wheel guide
17. Lockwasher
18. Guide screw

DT1 SERIES   RT1 SERIES
DT1MX, ALL   RT1MX, ALL
DT2 AND MX   RT2 AND MX
DT3   RT3
MX250   MX360

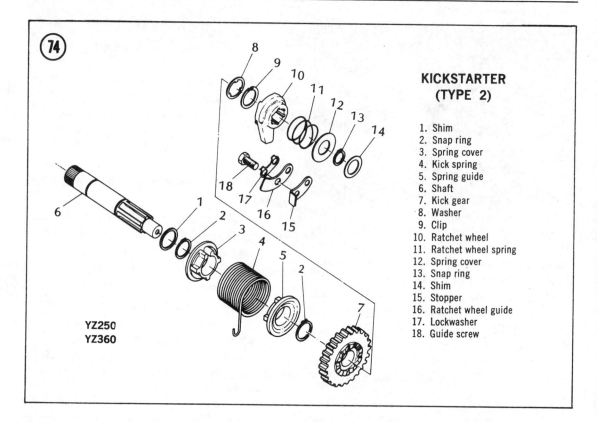

74

**KICKSTARTER
(TYPE 2)**

1. Shim
2. Snap ring
3. Spring cover
4. Kick spring
5. Spring guide
6. Shaft
7. Kick gear
8. Washer
9. Clip
10. Ratchet wheel
11. Ratchet wheel spring
12. Spring cover
13. Snap ring
14. Shim
15. Stopper
16. Ratchet wheel guide
17. Lockwasher
18. Guide screw

YZ250
YZ360

Service

The kickstarter is a simple, rugged mechanism. The cause of any malfunction will be obvious upon examination. Check that all parts move freely, and that gear teeth are not excessively worn.

Installation

Kickstarter installation is generally the reverse of removal. Observe the following notes.

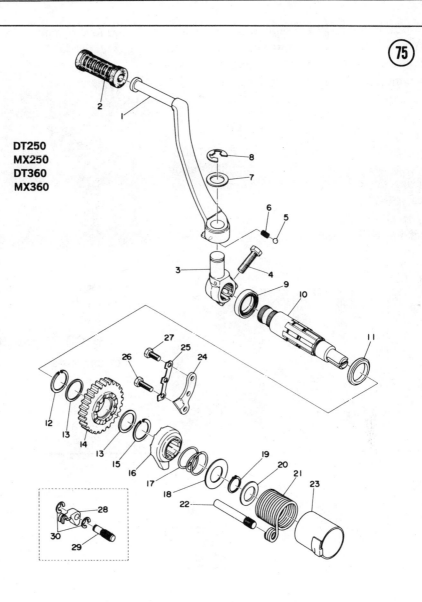

DT250
MX250
DT360
MX360

KICKSTARTER — TYPE 3

1. Kick crank
2. Kick lever cover
3. Kick crank boss
4. Bolt
5. Ball
6. Stopper spring boss
7. Washer
8. Circlip
9. Oil seal
10. Kick axle

11. Kick axle spacer (DT250)
    Plain washer (DT360)
12. Circlip
13. Gear hold washer
14. Kick gear
15. Circlip
16. Ratchet wheel
17. Ratchet wheel spring
18. Spring cover
19. Circlip

20. Gear hold washer
21. Kick spring
22. Kick spring stopper
23. Spring guide
24. Ratchet wheel guide
25. Lockwasher
26. Bolt
27. Bolt
28. Link (DT360)
29. Axle (DT360)
30. Circlip (DT360)

1. Be sure to install the shim mentioned under *Removal*, if your model is so equipped.

2. Insert the end of the kick shaft halfway into its bore, connect the spring, then push the assembly inward until it is fully seated.

TACHOMETER DRIVE

Figure 79 is an exploded view of typical tachometer drive gears. Refer to that illustration during removal and service. To remove these gears:

1. Remove retaining clip, thrust washer, and tachometer drive gear (**Figure 80**).

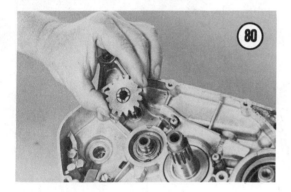

2. Remove retaining screw, retainer, and bushing (**Figure 81**).

3. Reverse the removal procedure to install the tachometer drive mechanism.

OMNI PHASE BALANCER

Some models are equipped with Omni Phase balancer, a device which minimizes vibration caused by reciprocating motion within the engine. **Figure 82** is an exploded view of this mechanism.

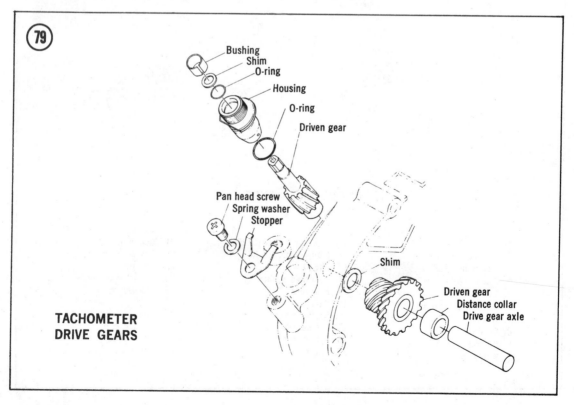

TACHOMETER
DRIVE GEARS

Bushing
Shim
O-ring
Housing
O-ring
Driven gear
Pan head screw
Spring washer
Stopper
Shim
Driven gear
Distance collar
Drive gear axle

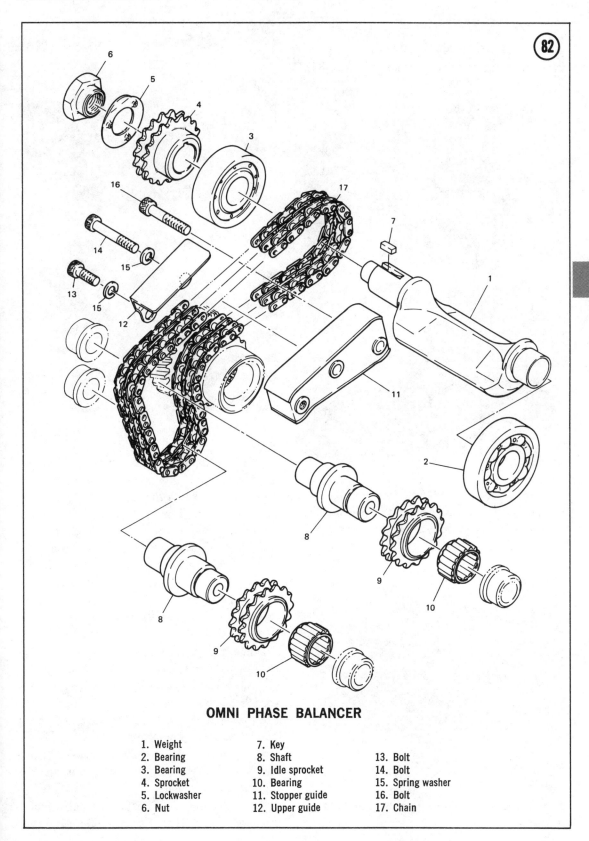

OMNI PHASE BALANCER

1. Weight
2. Bearing
3. Bearing
4. Sprocket
5. Lockwasher
6. Nut
7. Key
8. Shaft
9. Idle sprocket
10. Bearing
11. Stopper guide
12. Upper guide
13. Bolt
14. Bolt
15. Spring washer
16. Bolt
17. Chain

Removal

1. Remove chain guide (**Figure 83**).
2. Remove nut from rear sprocket (**Figure 84**).

3. Pull out shaft from upper front sprocket (**Figure 85**), then remove upper front sprocket.

4. Remove rear sprocket (**Figure 86**) and shaft key.

5. Remove lower front sprocket and chain (**Figure 87**).

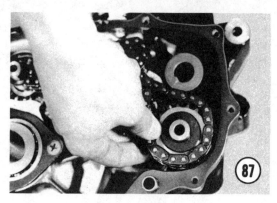

Installation

It is very important that the balance weight be properly phased with the crankshaft. There are timing marks on the rear sprocket and primary drive gear (**Figure 88**) to accomplish this purpose.

1. Slide rear sprocket onto its shaft, but do not install its retaining nut.

2. Install primary drive gear (**Figure 89**) if it was removed. Be sure to align punch mark on gear with punch mark, or gear with punch mark on end of crankshaft.

3. Align punch mark on rear sprocket with arrow mark on engine case (**Figure 90**).

4. Align punch mark on primary drive gear with arrow mark on engine case. Be sure that piston is at top dead center. If not, go back and check that Step 2 was done properly.

5. Place drive chain around lower front sprocket, then slip sprocket onto its shaft. No alignment is necessary.

6. Carefully loop drive chain around primary drive gear and rear sprocket. Be sure that

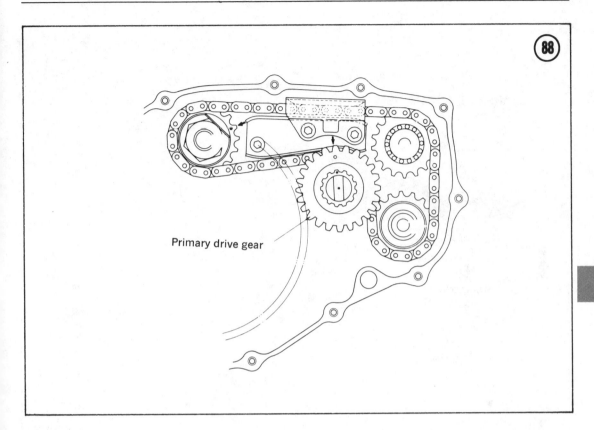

Primary drive gear

4

sprocket alignment is not disturbed during this step.

7. Place upper front sprocket into position, then insert its shaft through sprocket and into engine case.

8. Install rear sprocket lockwasher and retaining nut. Be sure to bend up tab on lockwasher.

9. Install chain guide.

10. Recheck all timing marks. If phasing is incorrect, vibration, poor performance, and early bearing failure will result.

SHIFTER

Figure 91 illustrates a typical gearshift mechanism. When the rider presses the gearshift pedal, the shaft turns, and moves the gear change levers. These change levers mesh with pins on the shift drum (part of the transmission). Therefore, as the pedal moves, the shift drum rotates. Grooves on the shift drum cause shift forks within the transmission to slide from side to side, thereby selecting the various gear ratios.

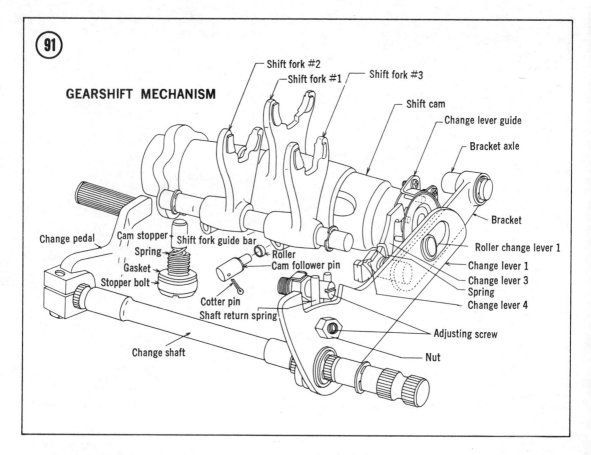

(91)

GEARSHIFT MECHANISM

Shift fork #2
Shift fork #1
Shift fork #3
Shift cam
Change lever guide
Bracket axle
Bracket
Roller change lever 1
Change lever 1
Change lever 3
Spring
Change lever 4
Adjusting screw
Nut
Change shaft
Shaft return spring
Cotter pin
Cam follower pin
Roller
Shift fork guide bar
Stopper bolt
Gasket
Spring
Cam stopper
Change pedal

Figures 92 through 101 (pages 61-70) are exploded views of shifters used on Yamaha 250-500cc singles. Refer to the applicable illustration during shifter service. Service procedures are generally similar for all models.

Removal (Types 1, 2, and 4)

1. Remove shifter shaft retaining clip and washer from left side of engine (**Figure 102**).

(102)

2. Pull shifter shaft and its attached change lever No. 1 out from right side of engine.

3. Remove change lever clip, then pull change lever from its shaft (**Figure 103**).

(103)

4. Remove retaining clip (**Figure 104**, page 71) from change lever No. 2.

5. Free hooks on change lever No. 3 from pins on shift drum, then pull change levers Nos. 1 and 2 free as an assembly.

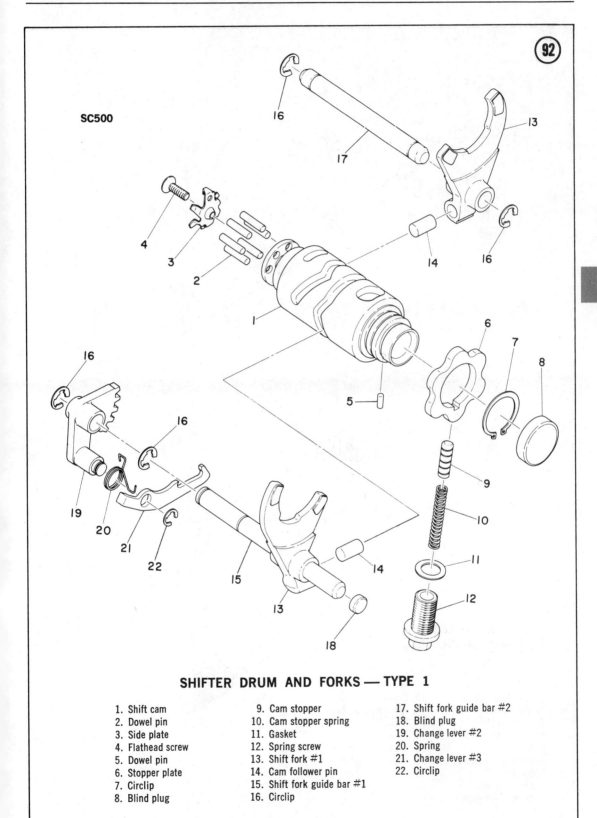

SC500

(92)

SHIFTER DRUM AND FORKS — TYPE 1

1. Shift cam	9. Cam stopper	17. Shift fork guide bar #2
2. Dowel pin	10. Cam stopper spring	18. Blind plug
3. Side plate	11. Gasket	19. Change lever #2
4. Flathead screw	12. Spring screw	20. Spring
5. Dowel pin	13. Shift fork #1	21. Change lever #3
6. Stopper plate	14. Cam follower pin	22. Circlip
7. Circlip	15. Shift fork guide bar #1	
8. Blind plug	16. Circlip	

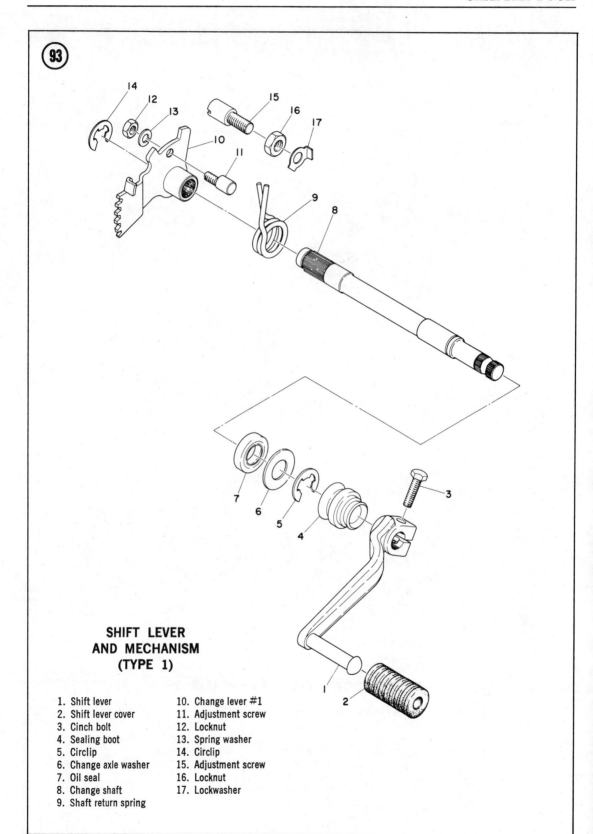

93

SHIFT LEVER
AND MECHANISM
(TYPE 1)

1. Shift lever
2. Shift lever cover
3. Cinch bolt
4. Sealing boot
5. Circlip
6. Change axle washer
7. Oil seal
8. Change shaft
9. Shaft return spring
10. Change lever #1
11. Adjustment screw
12. Locknut
13. Spring washer
14. Circlip
15. Adjustment screw
16. Locknut
17. Lockwasher

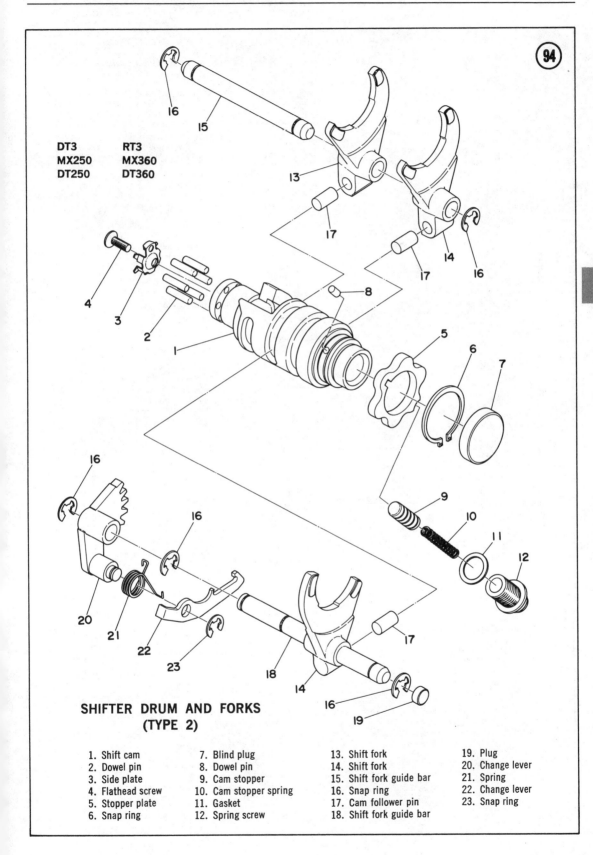

DT3 RT3
MX250 MX360
DT250 DT360

SHIFTER DRUM AND FORKS
(TYPE 2)

1. Shift cam	7. Blind plug	13. Shift fork	19. Plug
2. Dowel pin	8. Dowel pin	14. Shift fork	20. Change lever
3. Side plate	9. Cam stopper	15. Shift fork guide bar	21. Spring
4. Flathead screw	10. Cam stopper spring	16. Snap ring	22. Change lever
5. Stopper plate	11. Gasket	17. Cam follower pin	23. Snap ring
6. Snap ring	12. Spring screw	18. Shift fork guide bar	

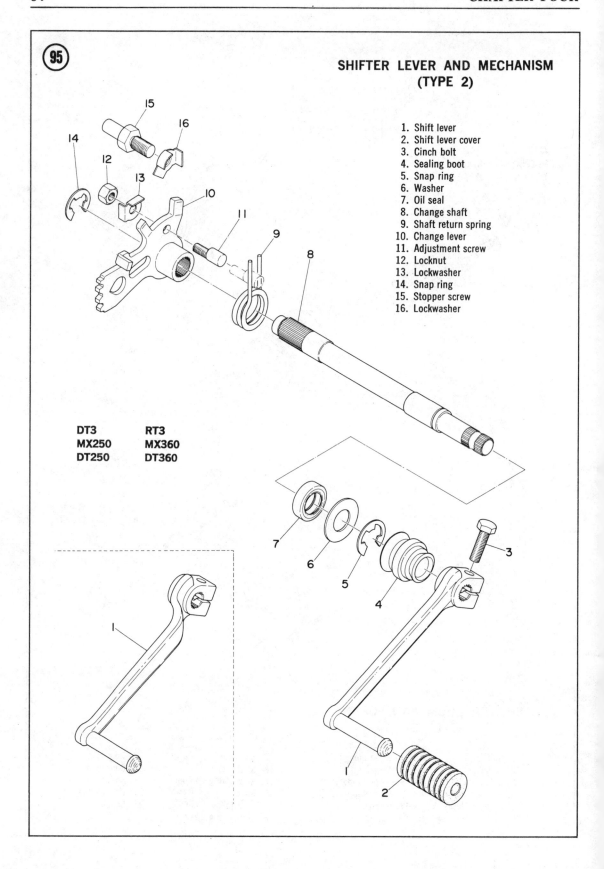

95

SHIFTER LEVER AND MECHANISM (TYPE 2)

1. Shift lever
2. Shift lever cover
3. Cinch bolt
4. Sealing boot
5. Snap ring
6. Washer
7. Oil seal
8. Change shaft
9. Shaft return spring
10. Change lever
11. Adjustment screw
12. Locknut
13. Lockwasher
14. Snap ring
15. Stopper screw
16. Lockwasher

DT3   RT3
MX250   MX360
DT250   DT360

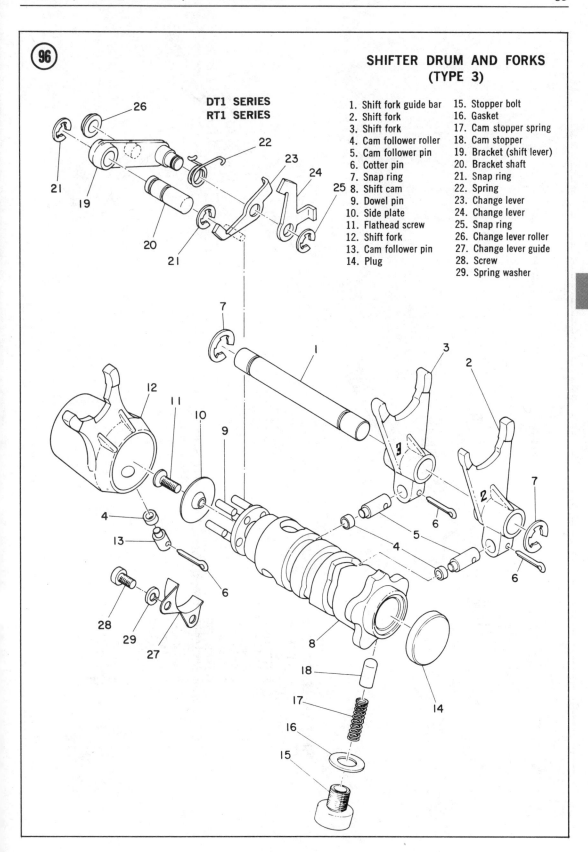

96

**SHIFTER DRUM AND FORKS
(TYPE 3)**

**DT1 SERIES
RT1 SERIES**

1. Shift fork guide bar
2. Shift fork
3. Shift fork
4. Cam follower roller
5. Cam follower pin
6. Cotter pin
7. Snap ring
8. Shift cam
9. Dowel pin
10. Side plate
11. Flathead screw
12. Shift fork
13. Cam follower pin
14. Plug

15. Stopper bolt
16. Gasket
17. Cam stopper spring
18. Cam stopper
19. Bracket (shift lever)
20. Bracket shaft
21. Snap ring
22. Spring
23. Change lever
24. Change lever
25. Snap ring
26. Change lever roller
27. Change lever guide
28. Screw
29. Spring washer

4

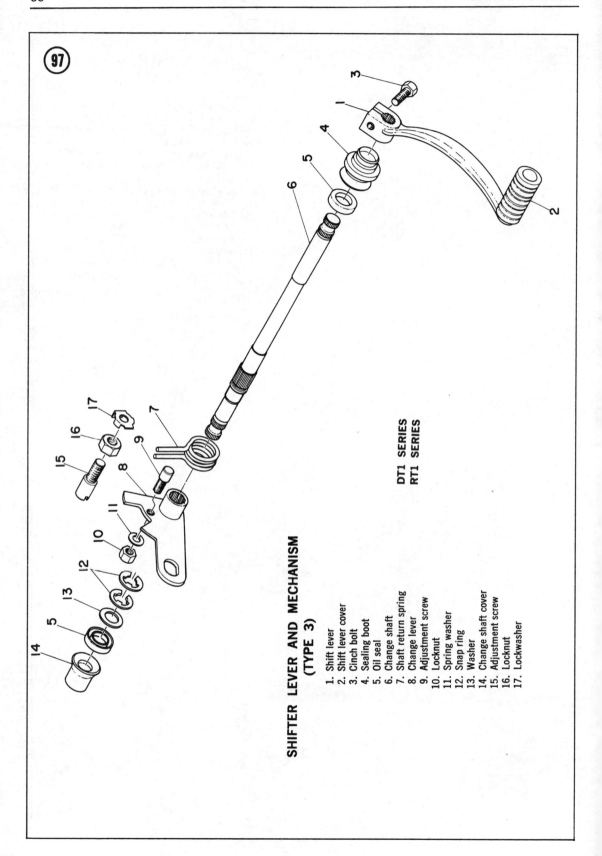

SHIFTER LEVER AND MECHANISM
(TYPE 3)

DT1 SERIES
RT1 SERIES

1. Shift lever
2. Shift lever cover
3. Cinch bolt
4. Sealing boot
5. Oil seal
6. Change shaft
7. Shaft return spring
8. Change lever
9. Adjustment screw
10. Locknut
11. Spring washer
12. Snap ring
13. Washer
14. Change shaft cover
15. Adjustment screw
16. Locknut
17. Lockwasher

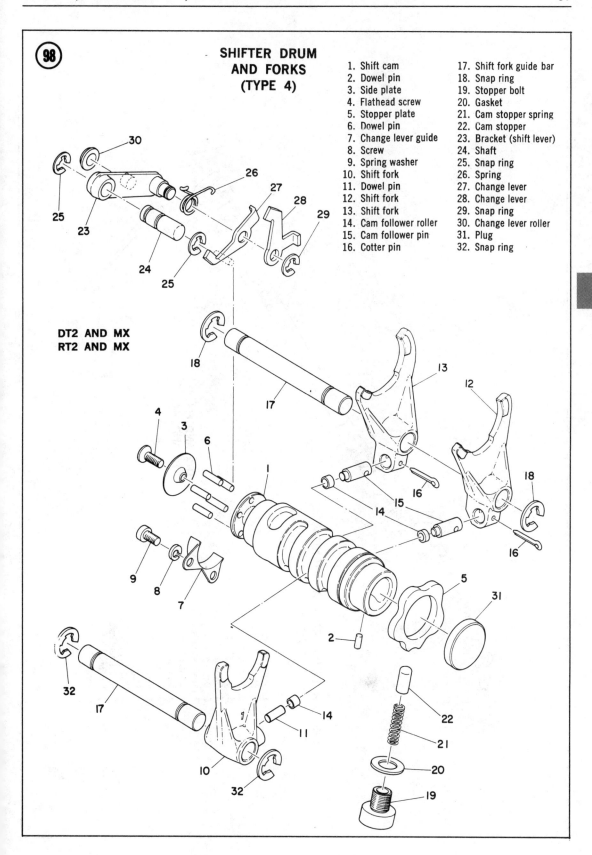

98

**SHIFTER DRUM
AND FORKS
(TYPE 4)**

1. Shift cam
2. Dowel pin
3. Side plate
4. Flathead screw
5. Stopper plate
6. Dowel pin
7. Change lever guide
8. Screw
9. Spring washer
10. Shift fork
11. Dowel pin
12. Shift fork
13. Shift fork
14. Cam follower roller
15. Cam follower pin
16. Cotter pin
17. Shift fork guide bar
18. Snap ring
19. Stopper bolt
20. Gasket
21. Cam stopper spring
22. Cam stopper
23. Bracket (shift lever)
24. Shaft
25. Snap ring
26. Spring
27. Change lever
28. Change lever
29. Snap ring
30. Change lever roller
31. Plug
32. Snap ring

**DT2 AND MX
RT2 AND MX**

4

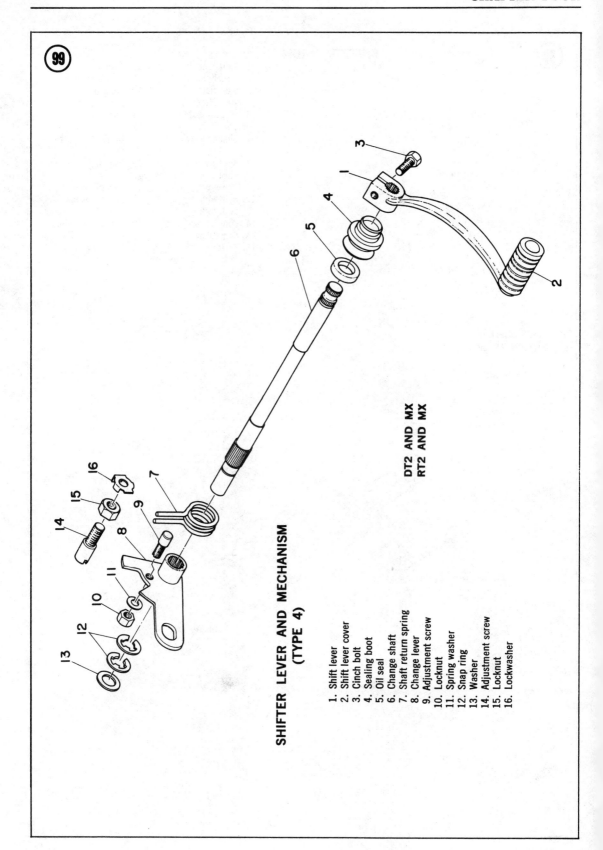

SHIFTER LEVER AND MECHANISM (TYPE 4)

DT2 AND MX
RT2 AND MX

1. Shift lever
2. Shift lever cover
3. Cinch bolt
4. Sealing boot
5. Oil seal
6. Change shaft
7. Shaft return spring
8. Change lever
9. Adjustment screw
10. Locknut
11. Spring washer
12. Snap ring
13. Washer
14. Adjustment screw
15. Locknut
16. Lockwasher

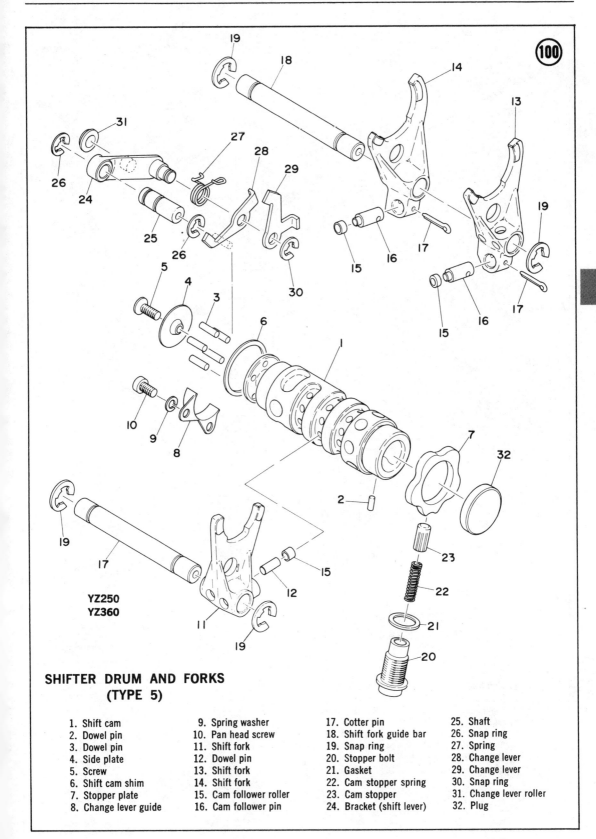

SHIFTER DRUM AND FORKS (TYPE 5)

1. Shift cam
2. Dowel pin
3. Dowel pin
4. Side plate
5. Screw
6. Shift cam shim
7. Stopper plate
8. Change lever guide
9. Spring washer
10. Pan head screw
11. Shift fork
12. Dowel pin
13. Shift fork
14. Shift fork
15. Cam follower roller
16. Cam follower pin
17. Cotter pin
18. Shift fork guide bar
19. Snap ring
20. Stopper bolt
21. Gasket
22. Cam stopper spring
23. Cam stopper
24. Bracket (shift lever)
25. Shaft
26. Snap ring
27. Spring
28. Change lever
29. Change lever
30. Snap ring
31. Change lever roller
32. Plug

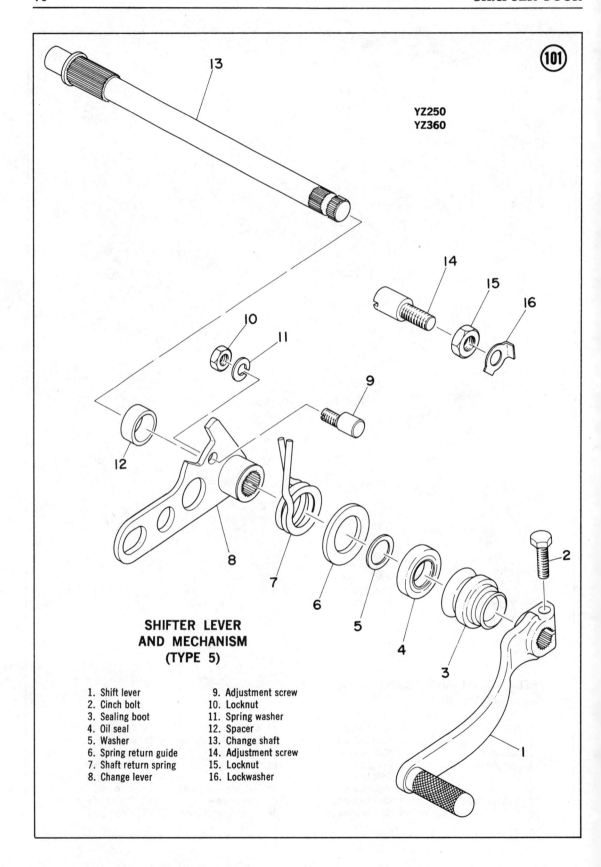

YZ250
YZ360

**SHIFTER LEVER
AND MECHANISM
(TYPE 5)**

1. Shift lever
2. Cinch bolt
3. Sealing boot
4. Oil seal
5. Washer
6. Spring return guide
7. Shaft return spring
8. Change lever

9. Adjustment screw
10. Locknut
11. Spring washer
12. Spacer
13. Change shaft
14. Adjustment screw
15. Locknut
16. Lockwasher

Installation (Types 1, 2, and 4)

Reverse the removal procedure to install this shifter. Note that gear teeth on change levers Nos. 1 and 2 must be aligned (**Figure 105**). Be sure to adjust the shifter after installation.

Removal (Types 3 and 5)

1. Remove shifter shaft sealing boot from engine left side (**Figure 106**).

2. Pull out shifter shaft and change lever No. 1 as an assembly (**Figure 107**).

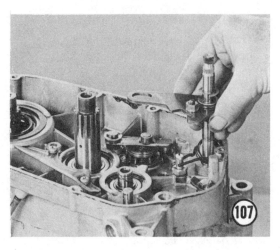

WARNING
The return spring may come off with this assembly. Remove it if it does, carefully; it is under tension.

3. Remove return spring (**Figure 108**).

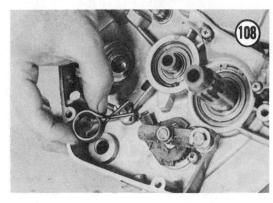

4. Remove roller from shift lever bracket.

5. Remove snap ring from bracket shaft, then remove bracket (**Figure 109**).

Installation (Types 3 and 5)

On these shifters, installation is the reverse of removal. Be sure to adjust the shifter after installation.

Shifter Inspection

Check return spring tension. Replace the spring if it is weak or cracked. Inspect the stop lever spring for cracks or weakness. Be sure that the return spring pin is not loose. If it is, missed shifts will result. Be sure that the locknut is tight.

Shifter Adjustment

The shifter must be adjusted under any of the following conditions:

   a. The transmission jumps out of gear.

   b. There is noticeable difference in shift lever travel between upshifts and downshifts.

   c. The shifter has been removed.

To adjust the shifter, refer to **Figure 110**, then proceed as follows.

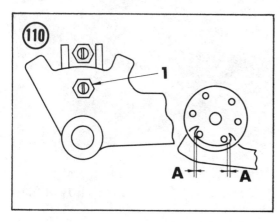

1. Loosen locknut (1).

2. Shift transmission to 2nd, 3rd, or 4th gear.

3. With no pressure on shift pedal, turn adjustment screw until distances (A) are equal.

4. Tighten locknut (1) slightly, enough to keep adjustment screw from turning.

5. Refer to **Figure 111**. Shift transmission to 3rd gear.

6. Shift back to 2nd gear. Hold arm against adjustment screw (2).

7. Measure gap (A).

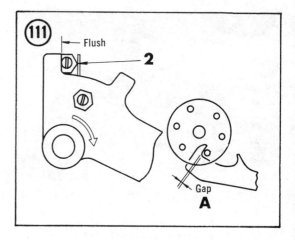

8. Shift transmission back to 3rd gear, then to 4th gear.

9. Again measure gap (A) when arm is held against adjustment screw.

10. If distances measured in Steps 7 and 9 are equal, no further adjustment is required; go on to Step 13. If distances (A) are not equal, loosen locknut (2), then turn adjustment screw until distances (A) are equal.

11. Tighten locknut.

12. Repeat Steps 1 through 3.

13. Tighten locknut (1).

CRANKCASE

The crankcase is made in 2 halves of die cast aluminum alloy. They are assembled without a gasket; only gasket cement is used as a sealer. Dowel pins hold the crankcase halves in alignment when they are bolted together.

Separating Crankcase Halves

At this point, very few parts remain attached to the engine. These parts must be removed prior to engine case separation.

1. Remove guide (**Figure 112**).

2. Remove shift drum stop (**Figure 113**). There is a steel plunger under the spring. Remove it with a small magnet.

3. Remove all assembly screws. Loosen them in a crisscross pattern, ¼ turn at a time, until all are loose, to prevent warpage. **Figure 114** shows sample locations, which differ depending on your model.

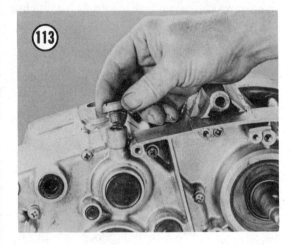

NOTE: *To prevent screw loss and to ensure proper location during assembly, draw a case outline on cardboard, then punch holes to correspond with screw locations. Insert removed screws in their appropriate locations.*

4. Install a crankcase separating tool, available at Yamaha dealers, on the right crankcase half. Be sure that both screws are in fully, then back

one out as required until the tool is parallel with the crankcase.

5. Rotate the crankshaft to top dead center, then slowly turn the puller screw clockwise until both cases begin to separate (**Figure 115**).

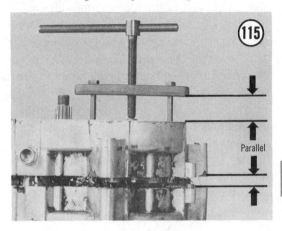

6. Using a rubber or rawhide mallet, tap the crankcase half as required, so that it does not tilt. Also tap the transmission shaft and shift cam, if necessary, to ensure that they remain in the left crankcase.

CAUTION
a. Crankcase separation requires only hand pressure on the puller screw. If extreme pressure seems to be needed, or if both case halves will not remain parallel, stop immediately. Check for crankcase screws not removed, shift linkage still attached, or transmission shafts hung up in bearings. Relieve puller pressure immediately.
b. Never pry between case halves. Doing so may result in oil leaks, or could possibly result in other damage.
c: Use only a rawhide or rubber mallet to tap case halves, and transmission shafts.

7. As you lift off the separated case, immediately check for transmission shims that may stick to the inside of the transmission bearings (inside the case). If a shim is lost, stop assembly until it is found or replaced.

Inspection of Case Halves

1. Clean both case halves thoroughly with solvent to remove dirt, oil, and metal particles.

Take particular care to prevent contamination of bearings.

2. Examine both crankcase mating surfaces carefully. Any damage to crank chamber sealing surfaces will result in lost crankcase compression and consequent poor running; other nicks or gouges in the transmission area may result in oil leaks.

3. Check that the transmission breather is not clogged. A clogged breather will result in pressure build-up and oil leakage.

4. Check crankshaft main bearings and transmission bearings for rust, wear, pitting, or excess radial clearance. If radial clearance of any bearing is more than 0.002 in. (0.05mm), replace the bearings. Before examining them, clean the bearings with solvent and dry them with compressed air.

CAUTION
Do not spin bearings with an air blast.

Transmission bearings are particularly susceptible to damage from metal particles or other foreign material in the transmission oil. Crankshaft bearings may become damaged if the air filter is damaged or missing. **Figure 116** illustrates a crankshaft bearing which failed after only a few miles of operation without an air filter.

Crankcase Assembly

1. Thoroughly clean both cases, then install transmission unit and crankshaft into the left case (see following sections on transmission and crankshaft for installation procedures).

2. Install all transmission and crankshaft shims.

3. Make sure all case locating dowel pins are installed, then place the right case down over the crankshaft and transmission shafts.

4. Apply sealing compound to both case mating surfaces. Follow the sealant manufacturer's application instructions. Place the transmission in NEUTRAL, then slide the right case half down into place, tapping it lightly, if necessary, with a rubber or rawhide mallet. If it does not seat easily, remove it, check for incorrect shim installation, or improperly installed parts.

5. Install all case screws. Tighten them in stages, in crisscross order, until all are firmly hand tight.

TRANSMISSION

Figures 117, 118, 119, and 120 are exploded views of transmissions installed in Yamaha models covered by this manual.

> NOTE: *Models with a similar type transmission have the same parts layout, but not necessarily the same dimensions or gear ratios.*

Models covered by this book are variously equipped with 4-, 5-, or 6-speed transmissions. Some gears are free to slide along splines on their respective shafts, and always turn with the shafts. There are dog clutches on these gears, which engage holes in other free-spinning gears. The splined gears are moved along their shafts by shift forks, which are controlled by a shift cam.

As one sliding splined gear is pulled out of engagement, because of shift drum rotation that moves the shift forks, another splined gear is pushed into engagement.

Neutral is established when the shift cam pulls all splined gears out of engagement simultaneously.

Figure 121 is a sectional view of a typical transmission. Arrows indicate movement of the various sliding gears within the transmission.

Removal

The following procedure applies to all models.

1. Support the left crankcase and hold the transmission assembly as shown in **Figure 122**. Using a rawhide or plastic mallet, tap both

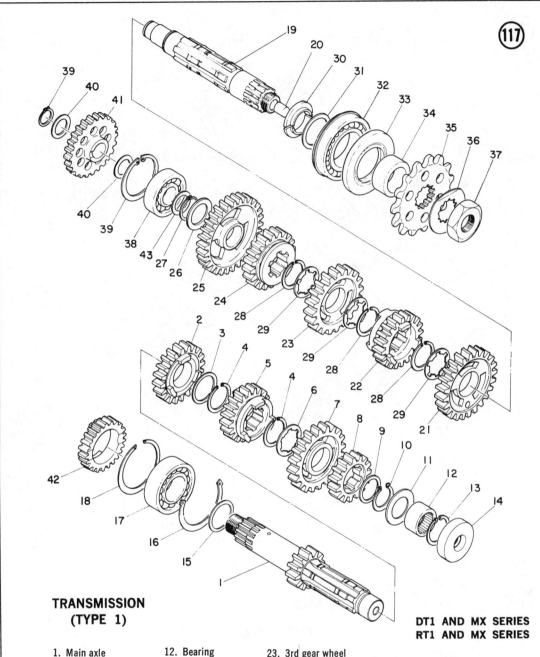

**TRANSMISSION
  (TYPE 1)**

DT1 AND MX SERIES
RT1 AND MX SERIES

1. Main axle	12. Bearing	23. 3rd gear wheel
2. 4th gear pinion	13. Circlip	24. 4th gear wheel
3. Washer	14. Oil seal	25. 1st gear wheel
4. Circlip	15. Main axle shim	26. Washer
5. 3rd gear pinion	16. Circlip	27. Circlip
6. Washer	17. Bearing	28. Circlip
7. 3rd gear wheel	18. Circlip	29. Washer
8. 2nd gear pinion	19. Drive axle	30. Spacer
9. Washer	20. Blind plug	31. Drive axle shim
10. Circlip	21. 2nd gear wheel	32. Bearing
11. Shim	22. 3rd gear pinion	33. Oil seal

34. Distance collar
35. Drive sprocket
36. Lockwasher
37. Locknut
38. Bearing
39. Circlip
40. Shim (outside case)
41. Kick idle gear (outside case)
42. Kick pinion gear (outside case)
43. Shim

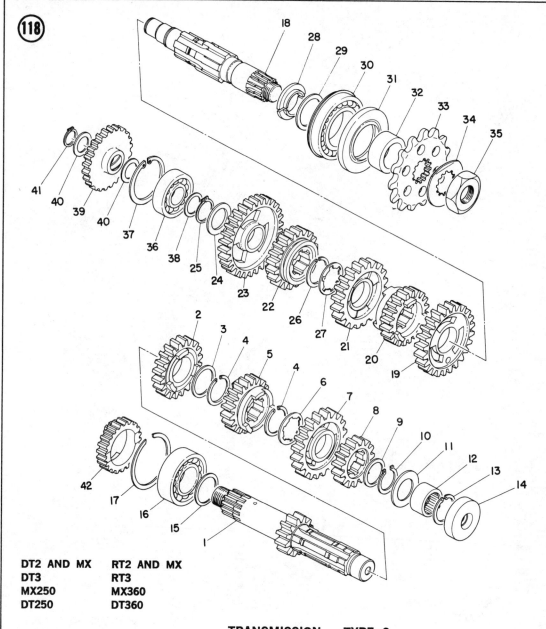

DT2 AND MX   RT2 AND MX
DT3   RT3
MX250   MX360
DT250   DT360

TRANSMISSION — TYPE 2

1. Main axle		22. 4th gear wheel	32. Distance collar
2. 4th gear pinion	12. Bearing	23. 1st gear wheel	33. Drive socket
3. Washer	13. Circlip	24. Washer	34. Lockwasher
4. Circlip	14. Oil seal	25. Circlip	35. Locknut
5. 3rd gear pinion	15. Main axle shim	26. Circlip	36. Bearing
6. Washer	16. Bearing	27. Washer	37. Circlip
7. 5th gear pinion	17. Circlip	28. Drive axle spacer	38. Drive axle shim
8. 2nd gear pinion	18. Drive axle	29. Drive axle shim	39. Kick idle gear (outside case)
9. Washer	19. 2nd gear wheel	30. Bearing	40. Shim
10. Circlip	20. 5th gear wheel	31. Oil seal	41. Circlip (outside case)
11. Shim	21. 3rd gear wheel		42. Kick pinion gear (outside case)

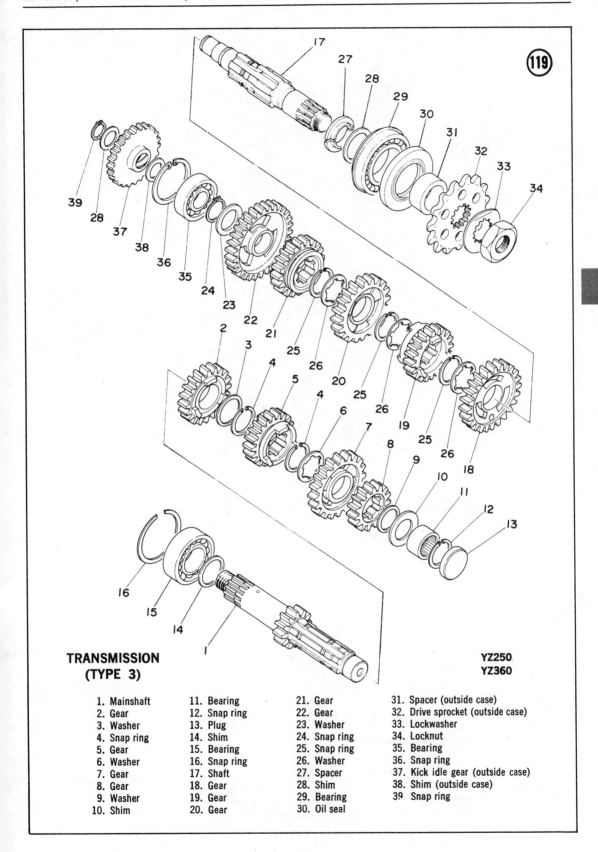

TRANSMISSION (TYPE 3)

YZ250
YZ360

1. Mainshaft	11. Bearing	21. Gear	31. Spacer (outside case)
2. Gear	12. Snap ring	22. Gear	32. Drive sprocket (outside case)
3. Washer	13. Plug	23. Washer	33. Lockwasher
4. Snap ring	14. Shim	24. Snap ring	34. Locknut
5. Gear	15. Bearing	25. Snap ring	35. Bearing
6. Washer	16. Snap ring	26. Washer	36. Snap ring
7. Gear	17. Shaft	27. Spacer	37. Kick idle gear (outside case)
8. Gear	18. Gear	28. Shim	38. Shim (outside case)
9. Washer	19. Gear	29. Bearing	39. Snap ring
10. Shim	20. Gear	30. Oil seal	

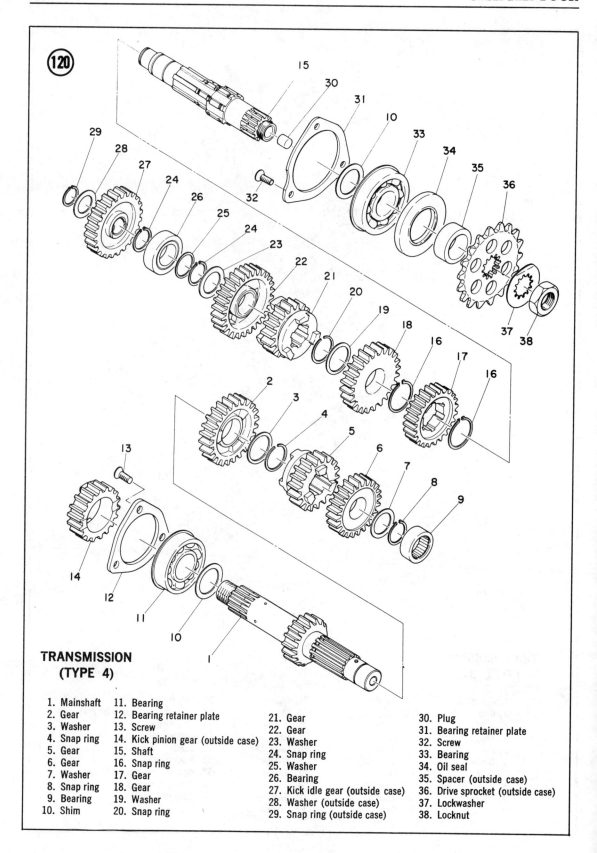

**TRANSMISSION
(TYPE 4)**

1. Mainshaft	11. Bearing
2. Gear	12. Bearing retainer plate
3. Washer	13. Screw
4. Snap ring	14. Kick pinion gear (outside case)
5. Gear	15. Shaft
6. Gear	16. Snap ring
7. Washer	17. Gear
8. Snap ring	18. Gear
9. Bearing	19. Washer
10. Shim	20. Snap ring

21. Gear	30. Plug
22. Gear	31. Bearing retainer plate
23. Washer	32. Screw
24. Snap ring	33. Bearing
25. Washer	34. Oil seal
26. Bearing	35. Spacer (outside case)
27. Kick idle gear (outside case)	36. Drive sprocket (outside case)
28. Washer (outside case)	37. Lockwasher
29. Snap ring (outside case)	38. Locknut

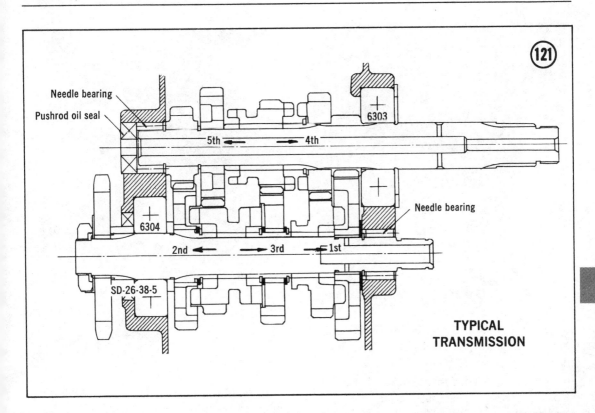

Needle bearing

Pushrod oil seal

5th ← → 4th

6303

6304

Needle bearing

2nd ← → 3rd ← 1st

SD-26-38-5

TYPICAL TRANSMISSION

4

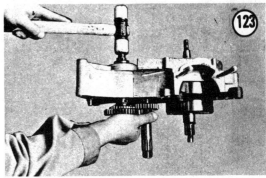

transmission shafts evenly from the case. Be sure to hold the entire transmission firmly to prevent parts from falling out prematurely. Take particular care not to let cam follower rollers (**Figure 123**) become lost.

2. As individual parts are disassembled, lay them out in order of their removal, and make a rough sketch of parts layout, if necessary. This procedure will greatly assist in transmission reassembly, especially if considerable time elapses before installation.

Inspection

1. Slide each splined gear along its shaft. Gears must operate smoothly. Minor roughness may be smoothed with an oilstone. Replace the gear and/or the shaft in the event of severe damage.

2. Check each gear for chipped or cracked teeth, or cracked wall sections. Replace any damaged gear.

3. Check dog clutches for rounded teeth, and also check that they engage properly. Replace gears with severely rounded clutch teeth.

4. Measure clearance between each shift fork and its associated gear (**Figure 124**). Any clear-

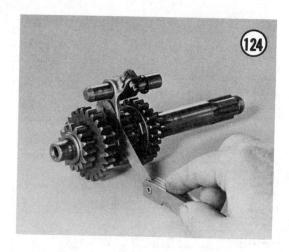

ance greater than 0.024 in. (0.6mm) is excessive. Replace the gear and/or shift fork in that event.

5. Be sure that shift forks are not bent or burned. Replace shift forks if their condition is doubtful.

6. Replace any shift fork guide bar that is bent. Roll it across a flat surface to check for straightness.

7. Mount each transmission shaft in V-blocks or other suitable centering device, then check it for straightness. Replace any shaft if it is bent more than 0.0008 in. (0.02mm).

8. Thoroughly clean transmission bearings, then oil them lightly. Rotate their inner races, and check them for rough operation. If any roughness is evident, and it cannot be eliminated by thorough cleaning, replace the bearing.

Installation

1. Assemble the transmission, shift forks, and shift cam into a single unit, as it was when it was removed.

2. Install the assembled transmission into the left crankcase. It may be necessary to tap it into place with a plastic or other soft-faced mallet.

3. On models with split keepers, a little heavy grease will hold these items in place during assembly (**Figure 125**).

End Play Adjustment

Whenever the transmission is disassembled, or it jumps out of gear for no apparent reason,

transmission shaft end play should be checked, and adjusted if necessary.

End play of both shafts must be 0.002-0.008 in. (0.05-0.20mm).

1. Main shaft end play is taken up automatically when the clutch retaining nut is tightened. If there was a factory installed shim on the right side of the main shaft, be sure that it is in place.

2. Measure across the entire width of the assembled countershaft, including all snap rings and existing shims. See **Figure 126**. Record this measurement as "dimension A".

3. Measure depth of each crankcase half, from its mating surface to the surface of the inner bearing race that supports the shaft (**Figure 127**).

4. From each measured depth, subtract the thickness of the parallel used to support the depth gauge. Call these measurements "dimensions B and C."

5. Add the depth of each crankcase half (dimensions B and C) to obtain the total distance between bearings when the crankcase is assembled.

6. Subtract assembled transmission shaft width (dimension A) from combined crankcase depth measurement. The difference between these measurements is shaft end play.

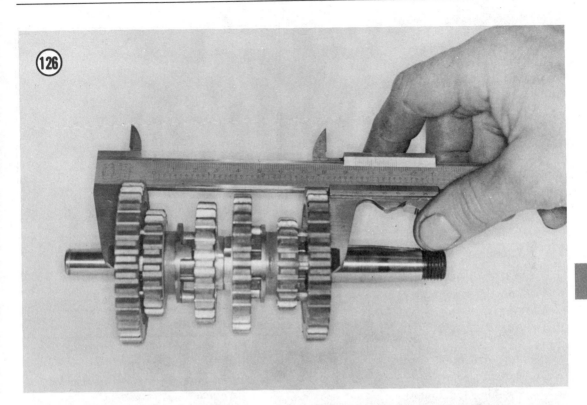

CHAPTER FOUR

Example:

   Width of shaft assembly:

     5.978 in. (151.85mm) (dimension A)

   Depth to left bearing,
   less thickness of parallels:

     3.748 in. (95.20mm)
    −0.750 in. (19.05mm)
     2.998 in. (76.15mm) (dimension B)

   Depth to right bearing,
   less thickness of parallels:

     3.750 in. (95.25mm)
    −0.750 in. (19.05mm)
     3.000 in. (76.20mm) (dimension C)

   Add dimensions B and C:

     2.998 in. (76.15mm)
    +3.000 in. (76.20mm)
     5.998 in. (152.35mm) (crankcase width)

   Subtract dimension A from
   total crankcase width:

     5.998 in. (152.35mm)
    −5.978 in. (151.85mm)
     0.020 in. (0.50mm) (total end play)

Desired end play is 0.002-0.008 in. (0.05-0.20mm). Therefore, to determine total additional shim thickness for that shaft, subtract desired end play, 0.004 in. (0.10mm) for example, from total end play:

     0.020 in. (0.50mm) (total end play)
    −0.004 in. (0.10mm) (desired end play)
     0.016 in. (0.40mm) (total shims required)

Add shims totaling 0.016 in. (0.40mm) to the shaft in question. Divide the shims equally on both ends of the shaft. Shims are available at Yamaha dealers.

CRANKSHAFT

The crankshaft operates under conditions of high stress. Dimensional tolerances are critical. It is necessary to locate and correct defects in the crankshaft to prevent more serious trouble later. **Figure 128** illustrates parts of a typical crankshaft assembly.

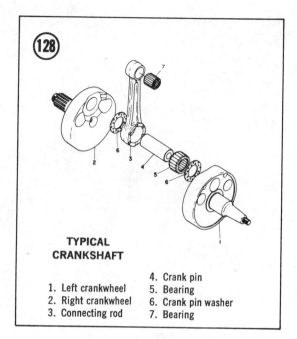

TYPICAL CRANKSHAFT

1. Left crankwheel
2. Right crankwheel
3. Connecting rod
4. Crank pin
5. Bearing
6. Crank pin washer
7. Bearing

CAUTION
Special tools are required to remove and install the crankshaft. Do not attempt service on this unit if proper tools are not available.

Removal

Start the crankshaft from the left crankcase, using the crankcase separating tool. Be sure that both bolts on the tool are fully tightened, and that the tool remains parallel to the crankcase, so that no side force is exerted on the crankshaft (**Figure 129**). Once the crankshaft is free from the left main bearing, lift it from the crankcase (**Figure 130**).

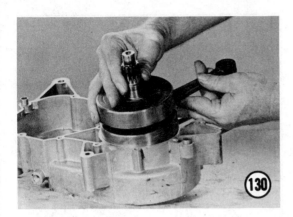

(130)

Inspection

There are several measurement locations on the crankshaft assembly. Measurements to be made are big end radial clearance, big end side clearance, and small end radial clearance.

Since it is difficult to measure big end radial clearance directly, measure the distance that the upper end of the connecting rod moves sideways when the lower end is held to one side (**Figure 131**). Side-to-side movement of the upper end should not exceed 0.079 in. (2.0mm).

NOTE: *Do not mistake lower end side play for upper end motion.*

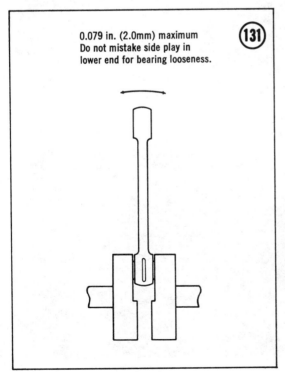

0.079 in. (2.0mm) maximum
Do not mistake side play in
lower end for bearing looseness.

(131)

Measure lower end side play as shown in **Figure 132**. Side clearance on a new or rebuilt crankshaft should be 0.016-0.020 in. (0.40-0.50mm). Rebuild or exchange the crankshaft if side clearance is 0.023 in. (0.60mm) or greater.

(132)

To measure small end radial clearance, clean and dry the piston pin, upper end bearing, and connecting rod. Assemble them without lubrication. Then check for any perceptible play in the upper end (**Figure 133**). If any exists, replace the piston pin and bearing. In extreme cases it may be necessary to replace the connecting rod.

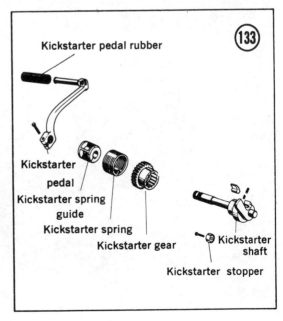

(133)

Kickstarter pedal rubber
Kickstarter pedal
Kickstarter spring guide
Kickstarter spring
Kickstarter gear
Kickstarter shaft
Kickstarter stopper

4

Crankshaft Runout

Mount the crankshaft in a lathe, V-blocks, or other suitable centering device. Rotate the crankshaft through a complete revolution and measure runout at the main bearing journals, as shown in **Figure 134**. If the dial indicator reading is greater than the repair limit, disassemble the crankshaft and replace the crankpin. If runout exceeds the standard limit, but does not exceed the repair limit, it may be corrected. Standard runout limit for all models is 0.0012 in. (0.03mm). The repair limit is 0.004 in. (0.10mm) for all models.

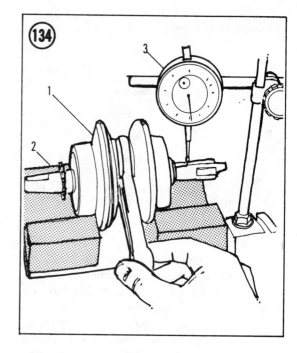

Crankshaft Overhaul

Crankshaft overhaul requires a press of 10-12 tons (9,000-11,000 kilograms) capacity, holding jigs, and a crankshaft jig. Do not attempt to overhaul the crankshaft unless this equipment is available.

1. Place the crankshaft assembly in a suitable jig, then press out the crankpin from the drive side first (**Figure 135**).

2. Remove the spacers, connecting rod, and lower end bearing (**Figure 136**).

3. Press the crankpin out from the magneto side (**Figure 137**).

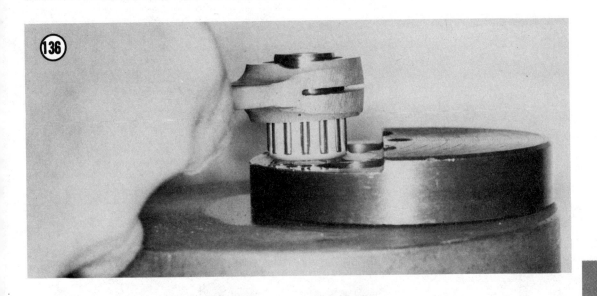

4. Carefully remove all residue from the crank wheels.

5. Using a suitable alignment fixture, press the replacement crankpin into the magneto side crank wheel (**Figure 138**) until the end of the crankpin is flush with the outside of the crank wheel.

6. Install a side washer, then the bearing.

7. Install the connecting rod, then the remaining side washer. There is no front or back to the connecting rod; it fits either way.

8. Using a small square for initial alignment (**Figure 139**), start pressing the drive side crank wheel onto the crankpin.

9. Insert a 0.016 in. (0.4mm) feeler gauge between the upper spacer and drive side crank

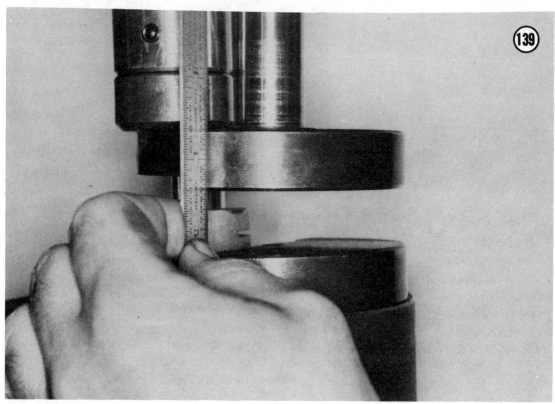

wheel. Continue pressing the drive side crank wheel onto the crankpin until the feeler gauge fits tightly.

10. Release all pressure from the press. The feeler gauge will then slip out easily.

11. Align the crankshaft assembly.

If, after a crankshaft seizure, either crankshaft half is damaged, replace entire crankshaft assembly. Otherwise, disassemble the crankshaft and replace the connecting rod, needle bearing, side washers, and crankpin.

Defective crankshaft seals are the most common cause of catastrophic crankshaft failures. Always replace crankcase oil seals when the crankshaft is removed for service.

Crankshaft Alignment

After any crankshaft service, it is necessary to align the assembly so that both crank wheels and the shafts extending from them all rotate on a common center. Mount the assembled crankshaft in a suitable alignment fixture, as described under *Crankshaft Runout*, then slowly rotate the crankshaft through one or more complete turns, and observe both dial indicators. One of several indications will be observed.

1. Neither dial indicator needle begins its swing at the same time, and the needles will move in opposite directions during part of the crankshaft rotation cycle. Each needle will probably indicate a different amount of total travel. This condition is caused by eccentricity (both crank wheels not being on the same center), as shown in **Figure 140**. To correct this situation, slowly rotate the crankshaft assembly until the drive side dial gauge indicates its maximum. Mark the rim of the drive side crank wheel at the point in line with the plungers on both dial gauges. Remove the crankshaft assembly from the jig, then while holding the magneto side crank wheel in one hand, strike the chalk mark a sharp blow with a brass or lead mallet (**Figure 141**). Recheck alignment after each blow, and continue this procedure until both dial gauges begin and end their swings at the same time.

2. After the foregoing adjustment is completed, the crank wheels may still be pinched, as shown in **Figure 142**, or spread (**Figure 143**). Both dial indicators will indicate maximum travel when the crankpin is toward the dial gauges if the crank wheels are pinched. Correct this condition by removing the crankshaft assembly, then drive a wedge or chisel between the crank wheels at a

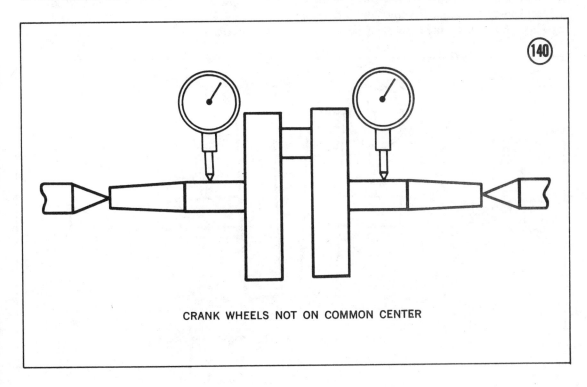

CRANK WHEELS NOT ON COMMON CENTER

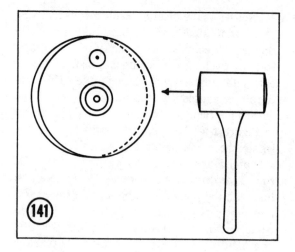

point opposite maximum dial gauge indication. Recheck alignment after each adjustment. Continue this procedure until the dial gauges indicate no more than 0.0012 in. (0.03mm) runout on each side of the crankshaft.

If the dial gauges indicate their maximum when the crankpin is on the side of the alignment test jig away from the dial gauges, the crank wheels are spread. Correct this condition by tapping the outside of one of the wheels toward the other with a brass or lead mallet. Recheck alignment after each blow. Continue adjustment until runout is within the tolerance specified in the foregoing paragraph.

NOTE: *It may be necessary to repeat the correction for eccentricity during the correction procedure for pinch or spread.*

BEARINGS AND OIL SEALS

Figure 144 illustrates typical bearings and oil seals. Always replace oil seals whenever the engine is disassembled.

Removal

Pry out the old oil seals with a screwdriver or similar tool. Place a piece of wood under the tool to act as a fulcrum and also to prevent damage to the engine case. Some models are equipped with seal retainers. Remove them (**Figure 145**) before prying out old oil seals.

Bearings are retained by snap rings. See **Figure 146**. There are also bearing retainer rings inside the case.

Heat crankcase halves to approximately 200°F (95°C), then turn each case over; bearings will drop out. If not, tap them lightly with a wooden mallet.

NOTE: *This temperature will damage rubber seals or plastic parts still attached to the engine. Have spares available.*

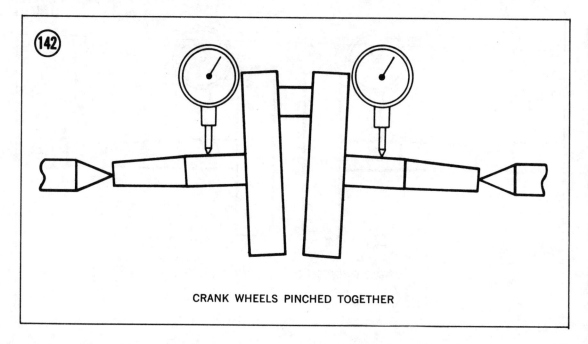

CRANK WHEELS PINCHED TOGETHER

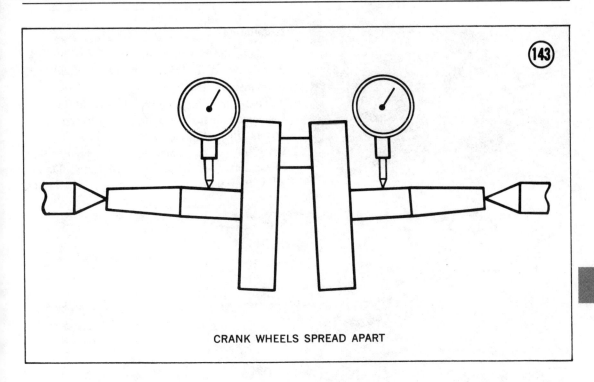

CRANK WHEELS SPREAD APART

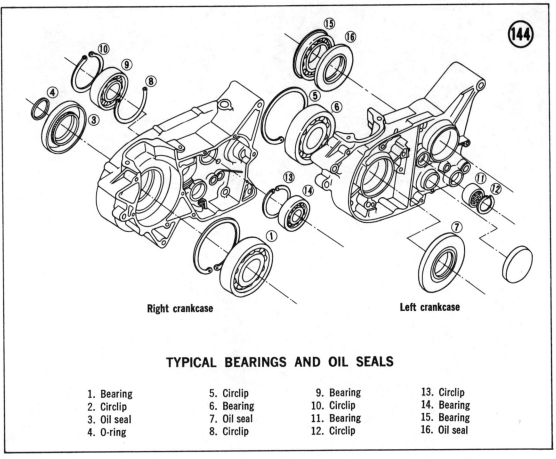

Right crankcase   Left crankcase

TYPICAL BEARINGS AND OIL SEALS

1. Bearing	5. Circlip	9. Bearing	13. Circlip
2. Circlip	6. Bearing	10. Circlip	14. Bearing
3. Oil seal	7. Oil seal	11. Bearing	15. Bearing
4. O-ring	8. Circlip	12. Circlip	16. Oil seal

Installation

Install the bearings and oil seals with markings outward. Lubricate the bearings with oil upon installation.

To properly install a seal, lightly oil the outer seal edge that slips into the hole. Tap repeatedly around the seal edge to start it into the hole. Once started, use a socket slightly smaller than the seal and tap the seal in until seated. Do not allow the seal to get cocked during installation.

CHAPTER FIVE

CARBURETORS

This chapter discusses carburetor operating principles, service, adjustment, and trouble-shooting.

CARBURETOR OPERATION

For proper operation, a gasoline engine must be supplied with fuel and air mixed in proper proportions by weight. A mixture in which there is an excess of fuel is said to be rich. A lean mixture is one which contains insufficient fuel. The carburetor supplies the proper mixture to the engine under all operating conditions.

Mikuni carburetors consist of several major systems. A float and float valve mechanism maintains a constant fuel level in the float bowl. The pilot system supplies fuel at low speeds. The main fuel system supplies fuel at medium and high speeds. Finally, a starter system supplies the very rich mixture needed to start a cold engine. Operation of each system is discussed in the following paragraphs.

Float Mechanism

Figure 1 illustrates a typical float mechanism. Proper operation of the carburetor is dependent on maintaining a constant fuel level in the car-buretor bowl. As fuel is drawn from the float bowl, the float level drops. When the float drops,

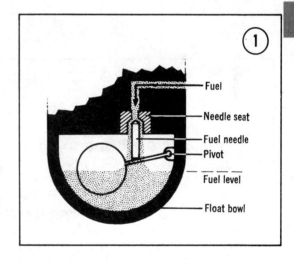

the float valve moves away from its seat and allows fuel to flow past the valve and seat into the float bowl. As this occurs, the float rises, pressing the float needle against its seat, thereby shutting off fuel flow. A small piece of dirt, trapped between the float needle and its seat, could prevent the valve from closing and allow fuel to rise beyond the normal level, resulting in flooding. **Figure 2** illustrates this condition.

Pilot System

Under idle or low speed conditions, at less than ⅛ throttle, the engine does not require

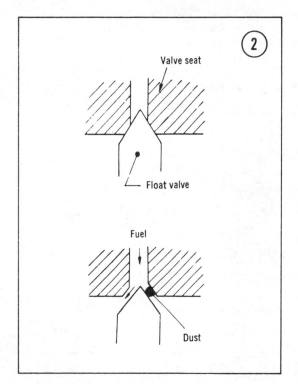

much fuel or air, and the throttle valve is almost closed. A separate pilot system is required for operation under such conditions. **Figure 3** illustrates pilot system operation. Air is drawn through the pilot air inlet and controlled by the pilot air screw. This air is then mixed with fuel drawn through the pilot jet. The air/fuel mixture then travels from the pilot outlet into the main air passage, where it is further mixed with air prior to being drawn into the engine. The pilot air screw controls idle mixture.

If proper idle and low speed mixture cannot be obtained within normal adjustment range of the idle mixture screw, refer to **Table 1** for possible causes.

Main Fuel System

As the throttle is opened still more, up to about ¼ open, the pilot circuit begins to supply less of the mixture to the engine, as the main fuel system, illustrated in **Figure 4**, begins to function. The main jet, needle jet, jet needle,

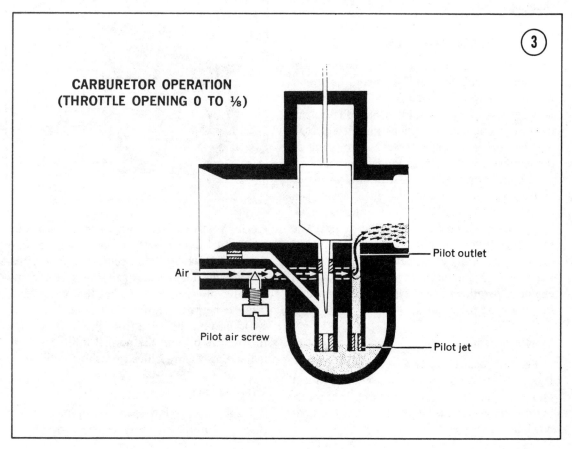

CARBURETOR OPERATION
(THROTTLE OPENING 0 TO ⅛)

Table 1   IDLE MIXTURE TROUBLESHOOTING

Too Rich
Clogged pilot air intake
Clogged air passage
Clogged air bleed opening
Pilot jet loose
Starter lever not returned
Starter plunger not closed
Starter cable misadjusted

Too Lean
Obstructed pilot jet
Obstructed jet outlet
Worn throttle valve
Carburetor mounting loose

and air jet make up the main fuel circuit. As the throttle valve opens more than about ⅛ of its travel, air is drawn through the main port, and passes under the throttle valve in the main bore. Air stream velocity results in reduced pressure around the jet needle. Fuel then passes through the main jet, past the needle jet and jet needle, and into the main air stream where it is atomized and then drawn into the cylinder. As the throttle valve opens, more air flows through the carburetor, and the jet needle, which is attached to the throttle slide, rises to permit more fuel to flow.

A portion of the air bled past the air jet passes through the needle jet bleed air inlet into the needle jet, where the air is mixed with the main air stream and atomized.

Airflow at small throttle openings is controlled primarily by the cutaway on the throttle slide.

As the throttle is opened wider, up to about ¾ open, the circuit draws air from 2 sources, as shown in **Figure 5**. The first source is air passing through the venturi; the second source is through the air jet. Air passing through the venturi draws fuel through the needle jet. The jet needle is tapered, and therefore allows more fuel to pass. Air passing through the air jet passes to the needle jet to aid atomization of the fuel there.

5

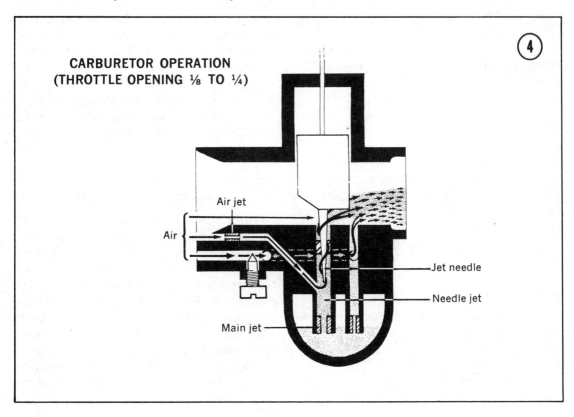

CARBURETOR OPERATION
(THROTTLE OPENING ⅛ TO ¼)

④

Air jet

Air

Jet needle

Needle jet

Main jet

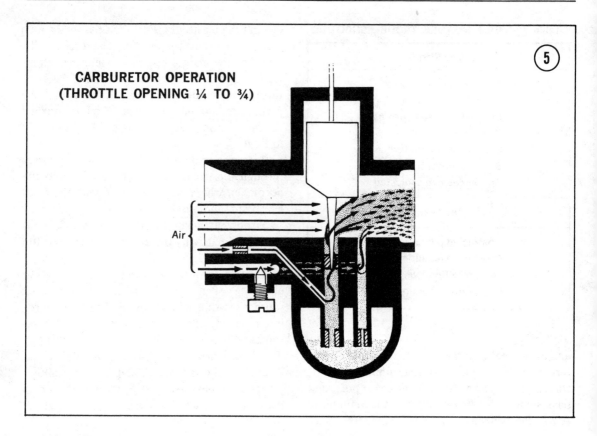

**CARBURETOR OPERATION
(THROTTLE OPENING ¼ TO ¾)**

Air

⑤

Figure 6 illustrates the circuit at high speeds. The jet needle is withdrawn almost completely from the needle jet. Fuel flow is then controlled by the main jet. Air passing through the air jet continues to aid atomization of the fuel as described in the foregoing paragraphs.

Any dirt which collects in the main jet or in the needle jet obstructs fuel flow and causes a lean mixture. Any clogged air passage, such as the air bleed opening or air jet, may result in an overrich mixture. Other causes of a rich mixture are a worn needle jet, loose needle jet, or loose main jet. If the jet needle is worn, it should be replaced; however, it may be possible to effect a temporary repair by placing the needle jet clip in a higher groove.

Starter System

A cold engine requires a fuel mixture much richer than that normally required. The starter system provides this mixture. A typical system is shown in **Figure 7**.

When the rider operates the starter lever, starter plunger (13) is pulled upward. As the engine is cranked, suction from the engine draws fuel through starter jet (10). This fuel is then mixed with air from bleed air port (11) in float chamber (12). This mixture is further mixed with primary air coming through air passage (14), and is then delivered to the engine through port (15) behind the throttle valve. Note that the mixture from the starter system is mixed with that from the pilot system.

CARBURETOR OVERHAUL

There is no set rule governing frequency of carburetor overhaul. A carburetor used on a street machine may go 5,000 miles or more without attention. If the machine is used in dirt, the carburetor might need an overhaul in less than 1,000 miles. Poor engine performance, hesitation, and little or no response to mixture adjustment are all symptoms of possible carburetor malfunctions. As a general rule, it is good practice to overhaul the carburetor each time you perform a routine decarbonization of the engine.

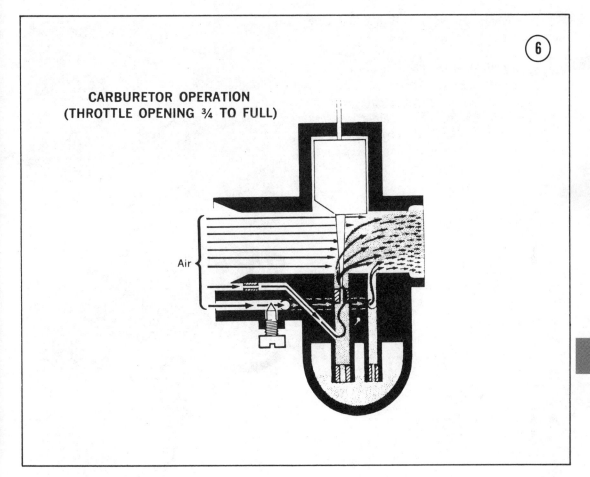

CARBURETOR OPERATION
(THROTTLE OPENING ¾ TO FULL)

Air

5

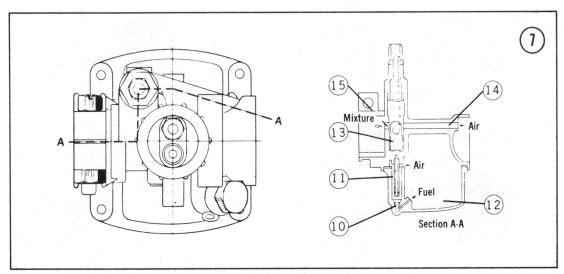

Section A-A

Remove the carburetor from the engine and disassemble it. Shake the float to check for gasoline inside. If fuel leaks into the float, the float chamber fuel level will rise, resulting in an over-rich mixture. Replace the float if it is deformed or leaking.

Replace the float valve if its seating end is scratched or worn. Press the float valve gently with your finger and make sure that the valve seats properly. If the float valve does not seat properly, fuel will overflow, causing an overrich mixture and flooding the float chamber whenever the fuel petcock is open.

Clean all parts in carburetor cleaning solvent. Dry the parts with compressed air. Clean jets and other delicate parts with compressed air after the float bowl has been removed. Use new gaskets upon reassembly.

CAUTION
Never blow compressed air into any assembled carburetor; doing so may result in damage to the float needle valve.

Always check float level after carburetor overhaul, and readjust if necessary. Refer to *Float Level*.

Mikuni carburetors are supplied as standard equipment on Yamaha motorcycles. They can be classified by float type; some models have independent floats, and others have single-unit, or twin floats.

Independent Float Carburetors

Figure 8 is an exploded view of this type carburetor. Refer to that illustration during disassembly and reassembly.

1. Remove mixing chamber cap (**Figure 9**).

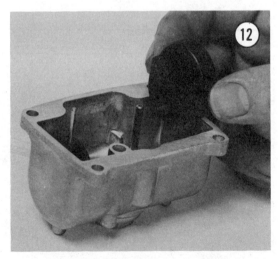

There is a spring under the cap; do not allow any parts to fly away.

2. Remove throttle slide assembly (**Figure 10**).

3. Remove float bowl (**Figure 11**).

4. Remove floats (**Figure 12**).

5. Remove main jet (**Figure 13**).

6. Remove pivot pin and float lever (**Figure 14**). Note carefully how float lever is installed; it is possible to reassemble this component upside down.

7. Remove float needle retainer, then float needle (**Figure 15**). Upon reassembly, install float needle retainer as shown in **Figure 16**.

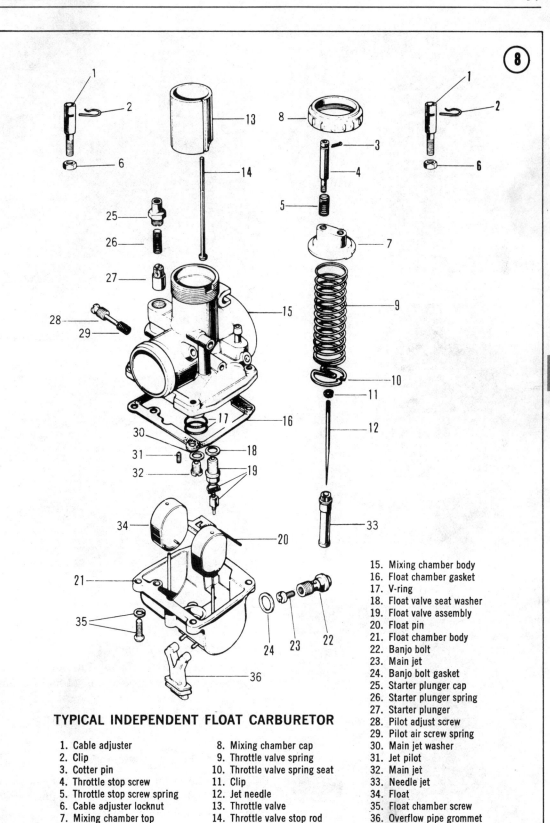

TYPICAL INDEPENDENT FLOAT CARBURETOR

1. Cable adjuster
2. Clip
3. Cotter pin
4. Throttle stop screw
5. Throttle stop screw spring
6. Cable adjuster locknut
7. Mixing chamber top
8. Mixing chamber cap
9. Throttle valve spring
10. Throttle valve spring seat
11. Clip
12. Jet needle
13. Throttle valve
14. Throttle valve stop rod
15. Mixing chamber body
16. Float chamber gasket
17. V-ring
18. Float valve seat washer
19. Float valve assembly
20. Float pin
21. Float chamber body
22. Banjo bolt
23. Main jet
24. Banjo bolt gasket
25. Starter plunger cap
26. Starter plunger spring
27. Starter plunger
28. Pilot adjust screw
29. Pilot air screw spring
30. Main jet washer
31. Jet pilot
32. Main jet
33. Needle jet
34. Float
35. Float chamber screw
36. Overflow pipe grommet

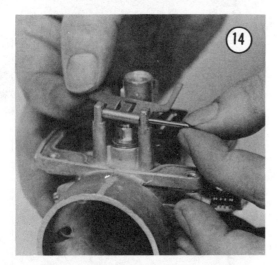

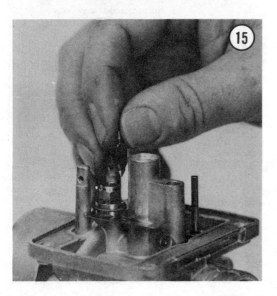

8. Remove float valve seat. If there is a plate underneath it, remove plate also (**Figure 17**). Note how washer is installed.

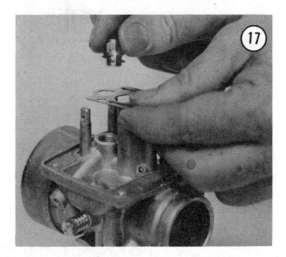

9. Remove pilot jet (**Figure 18**).

10. Invert carburetor, then push out needle jet (**Figure 19**). Do not use any metal tool for this operation.

11. Remove idle speed and mixture screws.

Single-unit Float Carburetors

Figure 20 is an exploded view of a typical carburetor of this type. Refer to that illustration during disassembly and reassembly.

1. Remove mixing chamber cap (**Figure 21**).

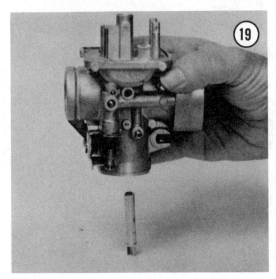

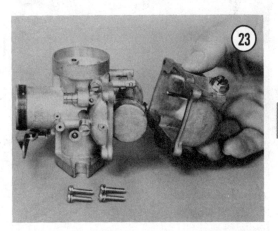

4. Remove pivot pin and float (**Figure 24**). Take care not to bend float assembly.

5. Remove float needle (**Figure 25**).

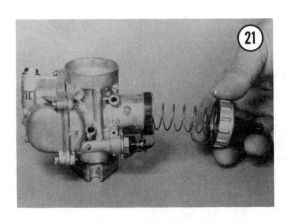

2. Remove throttle valve assembly (**Figure 22**).

3. Remove float bowl (**Figure 23**).

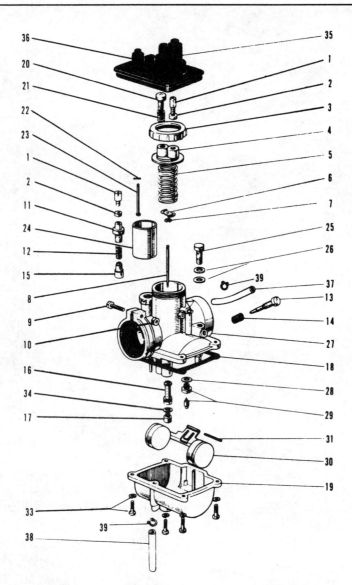

MIKUNI SINGLE FLOAT CARBURETOR

1. Cable adjuster
2. Cable adjuster lock nut
3. Mixing chamber cap
4. Mixing chamber top
5. Throttle valve spring
6. Throttle valve spring seat
7. Needle clip
8. Jet needle
9. Carburetor mounting clamp screw
10. Nut
11. Starter plunger cap
12. Starter plunger spring
13. Pilot air adjusting screw
14. Pilot air adjusting screw spring
15. Starter plunger
16. Needle jet
17. Main jet
18. Float chamber gasket
19. Float chamber body
20. Throttle adjuster
21. Throttle adjuster spring
22. Cotter pin
23. Throttle valve stop rod
24. Throttle valve
25. Banjo bolt
26. Gasket
27. Mixing chamber body
28. Float valve seat washer
29. Float valve complete
30. Float
31. Float pin
33. Float chamber fitting screw
34. Main jet washer
35. Carburetor cap grommet
36. Carburetor cap
37. Fuel overflow pipe
38. Air vent pipe
39. Circlip

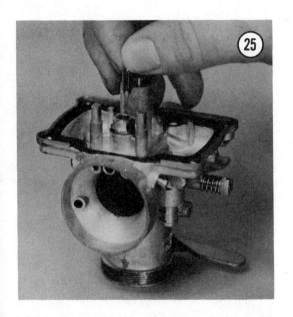

6. Remove main jet and its washer (**Figure 26**).

7. Remove float valve seat and its washer (**Figure 27**).

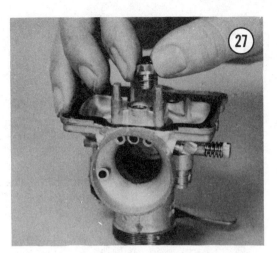

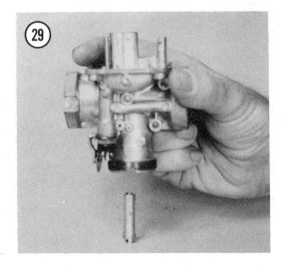

8. Remove pilot jet (**Figure 28**).

9. Push out needle jet, using a plastic or fiber tool (**Figure 29**).

10. Remove idle speed and idle mixture screws. Take care not to lose their springs.

CARBURETOR ADJUSTMENT

The carburetor was designed to provide the proper mixture under all operating conditions.

Little or no benefit will result from experimenting. However, unusual operating conditions such as sustained operation at high altitudes, or unusually high or low temperature, may make modifications to standard specifications desirable. The adjustments described in the following paragraphs should only be undertaken if the rider has definite reason to believe they are required. Make the tests and adjustments in the order specified. Float level should be checked each time the carburetor is disassembled, and adjusted if necessary.

Float Level

Mikuni carburetors with independent floats leave the factory with float levels properly adjusted. Rough riding, a worn needle valve, or a bent float arm can cause the float level to change. To adjust float level on these carburetors, refer to **Figure 30**, then proceed as follows.

1. Remove the float bowl and floats, then invert the carburetor body. Allow the float lever to rest on the needle by own weight.

2. Measure the distance from the float arm to the carburetor body surface.

3. Bend the tang on the float arm (**Figure 31**) as required for adjustment.

4. Float levels are specified in **Table 2**.

To adjust float level on carburetors with single-unit floats, refer to **Figure 32**, then proceed as follows.

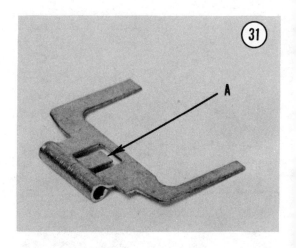

A. Bend tang to adjust float level

1. Remove the float chamber and invert the mixer body. Allow the float arm to rest on the needle valve by its own weight, without compressing the float needle spring.

2. Measure distance (A) from the top of the floats to the float bowl gasket surface. Note that distance (A) must be equal for each float.

3. Bend the tang on the float arm (**Figure 33**) as required for adjustment.

4. Float levels are specified in Table 2.

Component Selection

Figure 34 illustrates those carburetor components which may be changed to meet individual

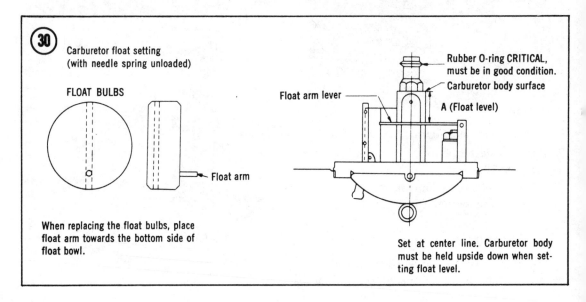

30

Carburetor float setting
(with needle spring unloaded)

FLOAT BULBS

Float arm

When replacing the float bulbs, place float arm towards the bottom side of float bowl.

Float arm lever

Rubber O-ring CRITICAL, must be in good condition.

Carburetor body surface

A (Float level)

Set at center line. Carburetor body must be held upside down when setting float level.

Table 2 FLOAT LEVEL

Model	Inch	Millimeters
DT1 series	0.59	15.1
DT1C-MX, DT1E-MX	1.00	25.5
DT2, DT3	0.59	15.1
DT2-MX	1.00	25.5
MX250	1.00	25.5
DT250	0.68	17.3
MX250	0.92	23.4
YZ250	0.92	23.4
RT1 series	0.33	8.5[1]
RT2-MX	0.33	8.5[1]
RT3	0.84	21.4[2]
MX360	0.33	8.5[1]
DT360	0.68	17.3[2]
MX360	0.92	23.4[2]
YZ360	0.92	23.4[2]

[1] Measured from carburetor body surface to float arm lever.

[2] Measured from base gasket surface to float arm lever.

A. Bend tang to adjust float level

test, operate the motorcycle at full throttle for at least 2 minutes, then shut the engine off, release the clutch, and bring the machine to a stop.

If at full throttle engine runs "heavily," the main jet is too large. If the engine runs better by closing the throttle slightly, the main jet is too small. The engine will run at full throttle evenly and regularly if the main jet is of correct size.

After each such test, remove and examine the spark plug. The insulator should have a light tan color. If the insulator has black sooty deposits, the mixture is too rich. If there are signs of intense heat, such as a blistered white appearance, the mixture is too lean.

As a general rule, main jet size should be reduced approximately 5 percent for each 3,000 feet (1,000 meters) above sea level.

Table 3 lists symptoms caused by rich and lean mixtures.

Adjust the pilot air screw as follows.

1. Turn pilot air screw in until it seats lightly, then back it out about 1½ turns.

2. Start engine and warm it to normal operating temperature.

3. Turn idle speed screw until engine runs slower and begins to falter.

4. Adjust pilot air screw as required to make engine run smoothly.

5. Repeat Steps 3 and 4 to achieve the lowest stable idle speed.

Next, determine proper throttle valve cutaway size. With the engine running at idle, open the throttle. If the engine does not accelerate

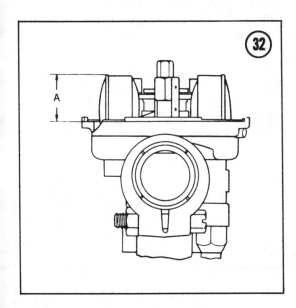

operating conditions. Shown left to right are the main jet, needle jet, jet needle and clip, and throttle valve.

Make a road test at full throttle for final determination of main jet size. To make such a

Table 3   MIXTURE TROUBLESHOOTING

Condition	Symptom
Rich mixture	Rough idle
	Black exhaust smoke
	Hard starting, especially when hot
	"Blubbering" under acceleration
	Black deposits in exhaust pipe
	Gas-fouled spark plugs
	Poor gas mileage
	Engine performs worse as it warms up
Lean mixture	Backfiring
	Rough idle
	Overheating
	Hesitation upon acceleration
	Engine speed varies at fixed throttle
	Loss of power
	White color on spark plug insulator
	Poor acceleration

smoothly from idle, turn the pilot air screw in (clockwise) slightly to richen the mixture. If the condition still exists, return the air screw to its original position and replace the throttle valve with one which has a smaller cutaway. If engine operation is worsened by turning the air screw,

replace the throttle valve with one which has a larger cutaway.

For operation at ¼-¾ throttle opening, adjustment is made with the jet needle. Operate the engine at ½ throttle in a manner similar to that for full throttle tests described earlier. To richen the mixture, place the jet needle clip in a lower groove. Conversely, placing the clip in a higher groove leans the mixture.

A summary of carburetor adjustment is given in **Table 4**.

MISCELLANEOUS CARBURETOR PROBLEMS

Water in carburetor float bowls and sticking carburetor slide valves can result from careless washing of the motorcycle. To remedy the problem, remove and clean the carburetor bowl, main jet, and any other affected parts. Be sure to cover the air intake when washing the machine.

Be sure that the ring nut on top of the carburetor is neither too tight nor too loose. If the carburetor mounting cinch bolt is loose, the carburetor can pivot, resulting in an improper mixture because the float level is changed.

If gasoline leaks past the float bowl gasket, high speed fuel starvation may occur. Varnish

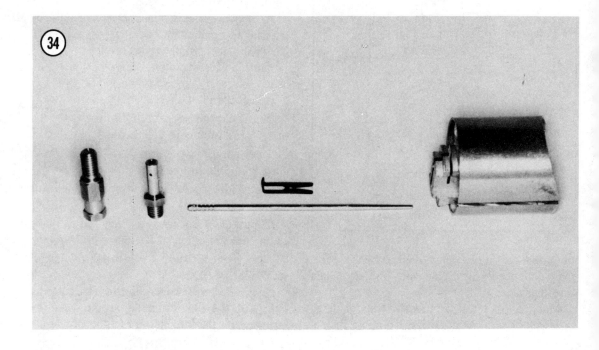

deposits on the outside of the float bowl are evidence of this condition.

Dirt in the fuel may lodge in the float valve and cause an overrich mixture. As a temporary measure, tap the carburetor lightly with any convenient tool to dislodge the dirt. Clean the fuel tank, petcock, fuel line, and carburetor at the first opportunity. Check the starter plunger occasionally, also. If the neoprene seal on the bottom is damaged, fuel will leak into the chamber and eventually work its way into the carburetor venturi, causing the machine to run rich.

Table 4   CARBURETOR ADJUSTMENT SUMMARY

Throttle opening	Adjustment	If too rich	If too lean
0 - 1/8	Air screw	Turn out	Turn in
1/8 - 1/4	Throttle valve cutaway	Use larger cutaway	Use smaller cutaway
1/4 - 3/4	Jet needle	Raise clip	Lower clip
3/4 - full	Main jet	Use smaller number	Use larger number

5

CHAPTER SIX

ELECTRICAL SYSTEM

This chapter discusses operating principles and maintenance of the ignition, lighting, and charging systems.

FLYWHEEL MAGNETO

Operation

A flywheel magneto provides electric power for the ignition and electrical systems of most of the models covered by this manual. Separate coils within the magneto supply current for ignition, daytime and nighttime operation, and battery charging. Alternating current produced by the magneto is used for ignition and lights, except for stoplights and turn signals. A rectifier converts this alternating current into direct current for charging the battery and operating the horn and turn signals. **Figure 1** illustrates construction of a typical magneto.

Figure 2 is a circuit diagram of a typical magneto ignition circuit. As the flywheel rotates, permanent magnets attached to the flywheel revolve past the various windings in the magneto, thereby inducing current in the windings.

When the contact breaker points are closed, the current (approximately 4 amperes) developed in the ignition coil is grounded, and no current is delivered to the ignition coil. When the points open, this current is delivered to the

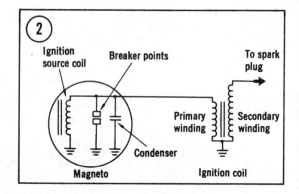

primary winding of the ignition coil. The 200 or 300 volts across the coil primary winding is stepped up to the very high voltage (10,000-15,000 volts) required to jump the spark plug gap. A capacitor (condenser) is connected across the breaker points. Action of the condenser assists the ignition coil in its task of developing the required high voltage, and also helps to prevent arcing and consequent burning of the breaker points.

Figure 3 illustrates a typical lighting and charging circuit. A portion of the current developed in the lighting coil is directed to the lighting circuits through the main switch; the remainder is used for charging the battery. The rectifier serves 2 purposes. It converts alternating current generated by the magneto into direct

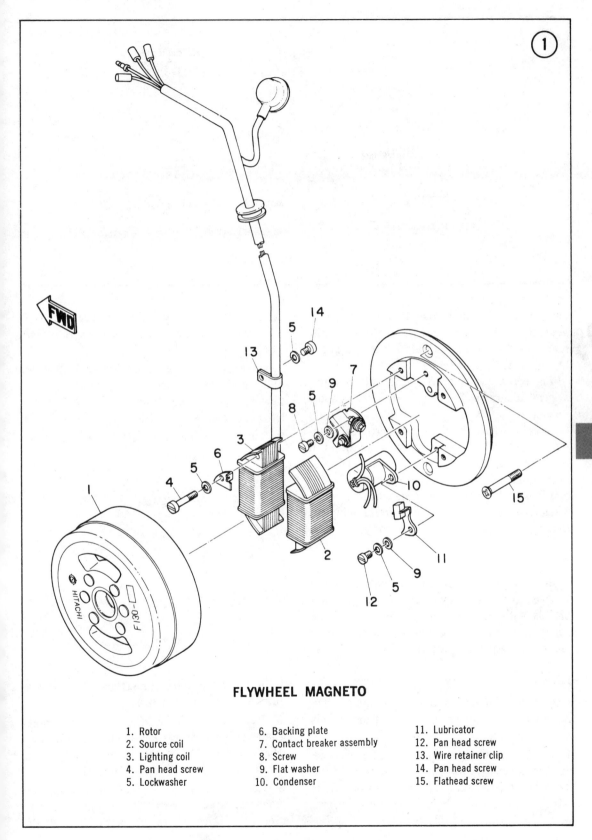

FLYWHEEL MAGNETO

1. Rotor
2. Source coil
3. Lighting coil
4. Pan head screw
5. Lockwasher
6. Backing plate
7. Contact breaker assembly
8. Screw
9. Flat washer
10. Condenser
11. Lubricator
12. Pan head screw
13. Wire retainer clip
14. Pan head screw
15. Flathead screw

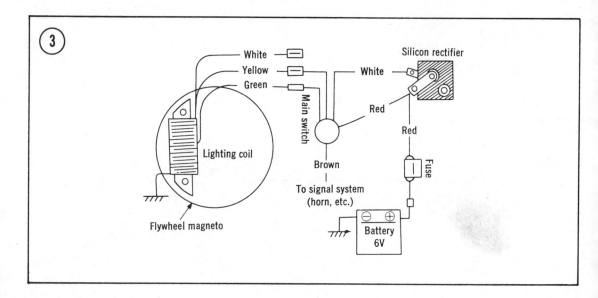

current for charging the battery, and it also prevents the battery from discharging through the magneto when magneto output voltage is too low to charge the battery.

Figures 4 and 5 are lighting and charging system diagrams for early and late model machines.

In cases where the battery is chronically undercharged, but otherwise in good condition, it is possible to increase its charging rate. Disconnect the green wire from the magneto where it connects to the green wire in the wiring harness. Then connect the white wire from the magneto to the green wire of the wiring harness.

Troubleshooting

In the event that an ignition malfunction is believed to be caused by a defective magneto on models with breaker points, check the coils, condenser, and breaker points as described in the following paragraphs.

Disassembly/Assembly

A flywheel puller is required for this job. Do not attempt to remove the flywheel unless this tool is available.

1. Remove flywheel retaining nut, flat washer, and lockwasher. A tool is available to hold the flywheel while its retaining nut is loosened. If this tool is not available, a strap wrench works well. Another method is to feed a rolled-up rag

between the primary reduction gears on the other side of the engine to prevent the crankshaft from turning.

2. Back out the screw fully from the flywheel puller body, then screw the puller fully into the flywheel center hole. Note that this hole has a left-hand thread.

3. Turn the puller screw clockwise to remove the flywheel (**Figure 6**).

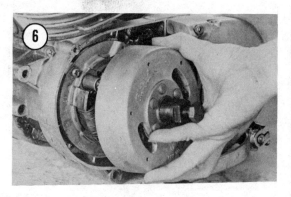

4. Remove the stator plate (**Figure 7**) after taking out its retaining screws.

5. Remove the Woodruff key from the crankshaft. To prevent this key from becoming lost, place it on one of the magnets inside the flywheel.

6. Reverse the foregoing procedure to install the magneto. Apply a very thin coating of distributor cam lubricant to the breaker cam inside the

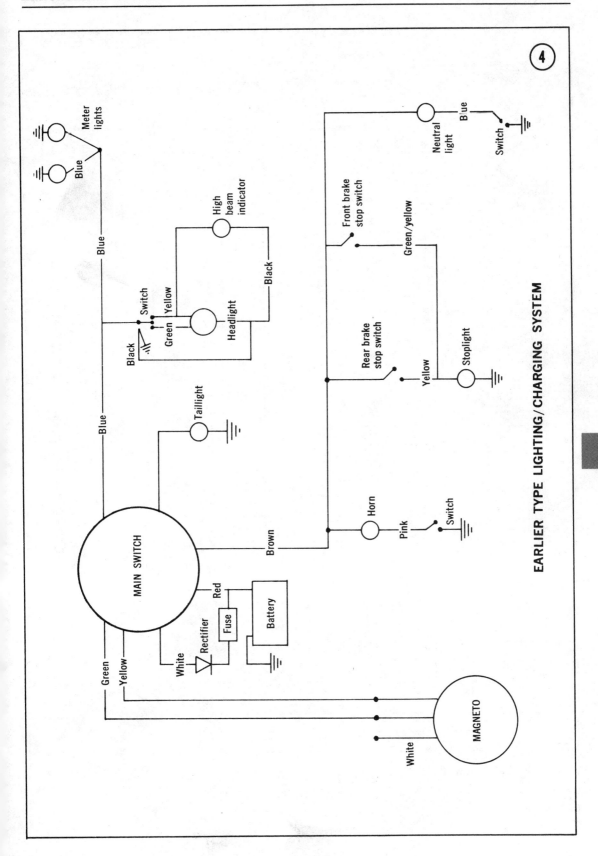

EARLIER TYPE LIGHTING/CHARGING SYSTEM

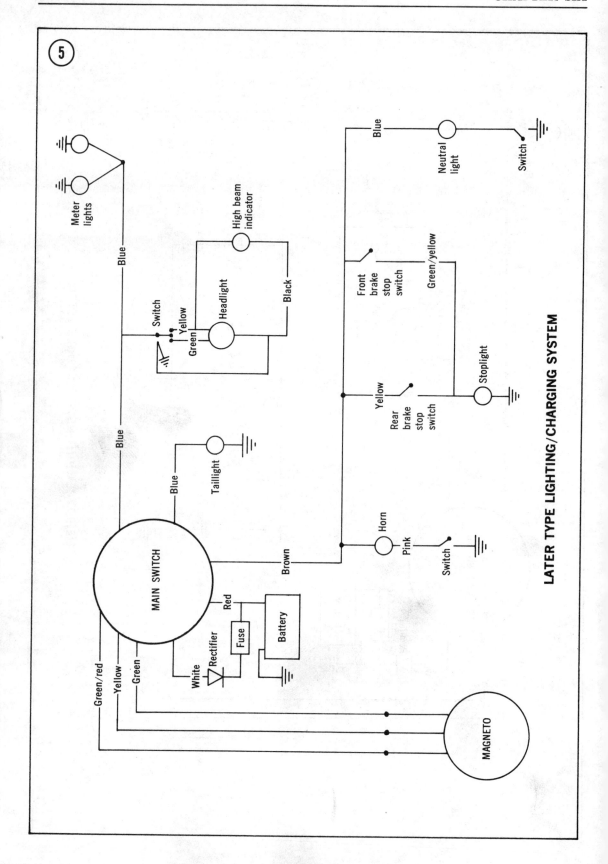

LATER TYPE LIGHTING/CHARGING SYSTEM

flywheel before installing the flywheel. Be sure that the Woodruff key is in place. Be sure to check ignition timing, and adjust it if necessary. Refer to Chapter Two for details.

Ignition Coil

With all magneto wiring disconnected, block the breaker points open with a piece of paper such as a business card.

Measure resistance between the movable breaker contact and ground with a low-range ohmmeter. If resistance is approximately 0.5 ohm, the coil is good.

If possible, disconnect the ground wire between the ignition coil and the magneto base. Measure insulation resistance between the iron core and the coil. Insulation resistance should be at least 5 megohms.

Condenser

Measure capacity of the condenser, using a condenser tester. Its capacity should be 0.18-0.25 microfarad. With the condenser ground wire disconnected, measure insulation resistance between the outer case and the positive terminal. Insulation resistance should be over 5 megohms.

In the event that no test equipment is available, a quick test of the condenser may be made by connecting the case to the negative terminal of a 6-volt battery, and the positive lead to the positive terminal. Allow the condenser to charge for a few seconds, then quickly disconnect the battery and touch the condenser lead to the case. If you observe a spark as the lead touches, you can assume that the condenser is good.

Arcing between the breaker points is a common symptom of a defective condenser.

Breaker Points

Refer to Chapter Two for details of breaker point service and ignition timing.

Lighting and Charging Coil

First be sure the battery is in good condition, then connect a 0-10 AC voltmeter between the yellow wire from the magneto and a good engine ground. Do not disconnect the yellow wire. Start the engine and turn on the lights. Run the engine at 2,500 rpm. The voltmeter must indicate at least 5.0 volts. Then increase engine speed to 8,000 rpm long enough to read the meter. The voltmeter must indicate not greater than 8.0 volts.

If the measurements obtained were not within specifications, check for poor connections or chafed wiring in the lighting and charging circuit. Refer back to Figure 4 or 5 as necessary to trace the circuits involved.

Charging Circuit Test (Early Models)

Before checking the charging system, be sure the battery is in good condition, and that it is fully charged. The following checks will not be meaningful if the battery is low or defective.

Connect the positive terminal of a 0-10 DC voltmeter to the positive battery lead (red), and the negative voltmeter terminal to a good engine ground. Start the engine and run it under the conditions specified in **Table 1**.

Table 1   OUTPUT VOLTAGE

RPM	Voltage	Remarks
2,500	5.0 or greater	Lights on
8,000	8.0 or less	Lights on

With the engine not running, disconnect the red wire at the battery. Connect the positive terminal of a 0-5 DC ammeter to the wire which was disconnected. Connect the negative ammeter terminal to the positive battery terminal. Start the engine, then slowly increase rpm to 2,500. At this speed, the ammeter should show a slight charging current. Momentarily increase engine speed to 8,000 rpm. At this speed, charging current should not exceed 2.0 amperes.

If the charging system does not meet specifications, check all wiring, connections, magneto charging coil, main switch, and the rectifier.

Charging Circuit Test (Late Models)

Before checking the charging system, be sure that the battery is in good condition, and that it is fully charged. The following checks will not be meaningful if the battery is low or defective.

Connect the positive terminal of a 0-10 DC voltmeter to the positive battery lead (red), and the negative voltmeter terminal to a good engine ground. Start the engine and run it under the conditions listed in **Table 2**.

Table 2   CHARGING VOLTAGE

RPM	Voltage	
	Day	Night
2,000	8.0 ± 0.5	8.5 ± 0.5
8,000	8.5 ± 0.5	8.5 ± 0.5

With the engine not running, disconnect the red wire at the battery. Connect the positive terminal of a 0-5 DC ammeter to the wire which was disconnected. Connect the negative ammeter terminal to the positive battery terminal. Start the engine, then run it under each of the conditions listed in **Table 3**.

Table 3   CHARGING CIRCUIT

RPM	Voltage	
	Day	Night
2,000	1.8 ± 0.5	0.7 ± 0.5
8,000	3.0 ± 0.5	1.5 ± 0.5

If the charging circuit does not meet specifications, check all wiring, charging coil, connections, main switch, and rectifier.

Rectifier

The rectifier serves 2 purposes. It converts alternating current produced by the magneto into direct current for charging the battery, and also prevents discharge of the battery through the magneto when the engine is not running, or at other times when magneto voltage is less than that of the battery.

To check the rectifier, measure its resistance in both forward and reverse directions. Resistance in one direction should be approximately 10 ohms. In the reverse direction, resistance should be essentially infinite (**Figure 8**). Never connect the rectifier directly to the battery to make a continuity check; doing so will cause instantaneous damage.

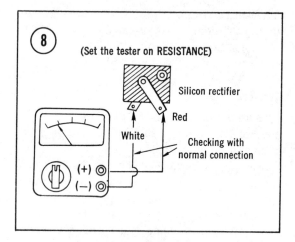

(Set the tester on RESISTANCE)

Silicon rectifier
Red
White
Checking with normal connection

(+)
(−)

CAPACITOR DISCHARGE IGNITION (CDI)

Some models are equipped with electronic ignition. This solid-state system, unlike conventional magneto ignition, has no breaker points or other moving parts. Yamaha electronic ignition may be classified as inner- and outer-rotor systems. Wiring of each system is different, but their operation is otherwise similar.

Figures 9 and 10 are exploded views of the magnetos for these systems. **Figures 11 and 12** illustrate system connections.

Other than keeping system electrical connections clean and tight, no maintenance is required.

In the event of CDI malfunction, a few checks may be made with an ohmmeter. **Table 4** lists test points and approximate resistance values to be obtained. In the event that these checks do not reveal the problem, take the bike to a Yamaha dealer who has a CDI tester.

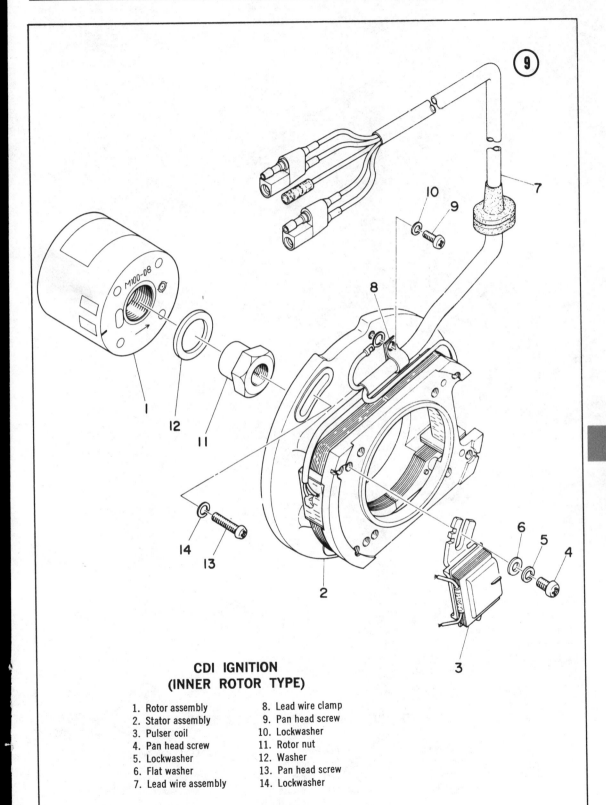

CDI IGNITION
(INNER ROTOR TYPE)

1. Rotor assembly
2. Stator assembly
3. Pulser coil
4. Pan head screw
5. Lockwasher
6. Flat washer
7. Lead wire assembly
8. Lead wire clamp
9. Pan head screw
10. Lockwasher
11. Rotor nut
12. Washer
13. Pan head screw
14. Lockwasher

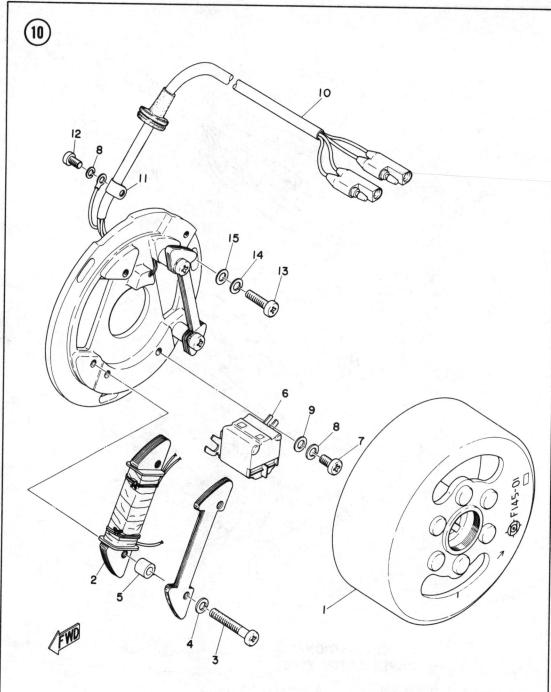

CDI IGNITION – OUTER ROTOR TYPE

1. Rotor assembly	6. Pulser coil	11. Lead wire clamp
2. Source coil	7. Pan head screw	12. Screw
3. Pan head screw	8. Lockwasher	13. Pan head screw
4. Lockwasher	9. Flat washer	14. Lockwasher
5. Spacer	10. Lead wire assembly	15. Flat washer

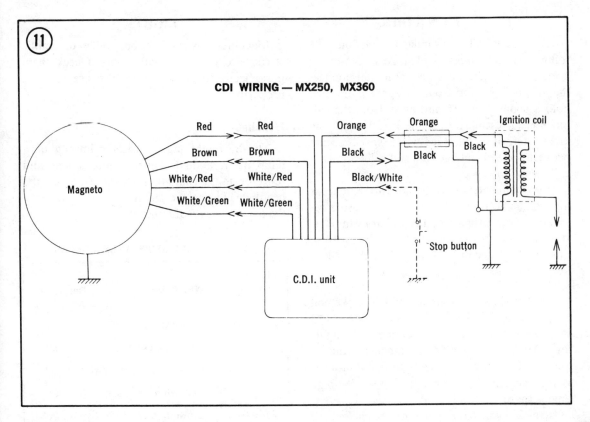

CDI WIRING — MX250, MX360

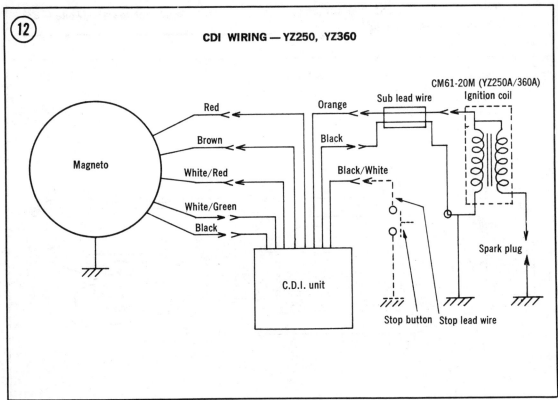

CDI WIRING — YZ250, YZ360

6

IGNITION COIL

All ignition coils are similar in function. The following checks apply to all models.

As a quick check of coil condition, disconnect the high voltage lead from the spark plug, then hold it about ¼ in. (6mm) away from the cylinder head. Crank the engine briskly with the kickstarter. If a fat, blue-white spark occurs between the high voltage lead and cylinder head, coil condition is good.

If an ohmmeter is available, further checks may be made. Refer to **Figure 13**. Measure resistance of coil primary and secondary windings. If measurements are appreciably different from those values listed in **Table 5**, replace the coil.

CHOKE COIL

Some models are equipped with a choke coil in the night lighting circuit. As engine speed increases, so does output frequency of the lighting current developed in the magneto. Inductance of the choke coil tends to maintain current to the lights at a more constant level at high engine speed.

No maintenance is required on the choke coil. If its condition is doubtful, check it for continuity and insulation from ground.

LIGHTS

Machines designed to be ridden on public streets are equipped with lights. Check them periodically to be sure that they are working properly.

Headlight

The headlight unit consists primarily of a lamp body, a dual-filament bulb, a lens and reflector unit, a rim, and a socket. To adjust the headlight, loosen the mounting bolts and move the assembly as required.

Table 4   CDI RESISTANCE CHECKS

Magneto Model	Wire Colors	Resistance
M100-08	Brown to black	790
	Red to black	85
	Red/white to green/white	50
	Red/white to black	0
F145-01	Brown to black	205
	Red/white to green/white	85

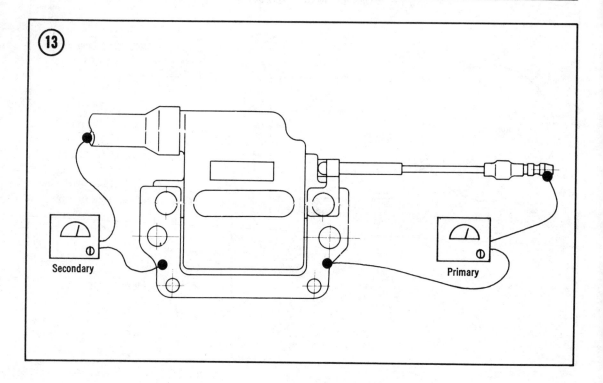

Table 5   IGNITION COIL CHECKS

Model	Primary Resistance	Secondary Resistance
DT1 series	0.6	6,000
DT2	0.9	6,500
DT3	0.6	6,000
DT2-MX	1.7	6,000
MX250	1.0	6,000
DT250	0.6	6,000
MX250	0.6	6,000
YZ250	0.6	6,000
RT1 series	0.6	6,000
RT2	0.9	6,500
RT2-MX	1.7	6,000
RT3	0.6	6,000
MX360	0.6	6,000
DT360	0.6	6,000
YZ360	0.6	6,000
DT400	0.6	6,000

NOTE: Disconnect spark plug cap from cable before measuring secondary resistance.

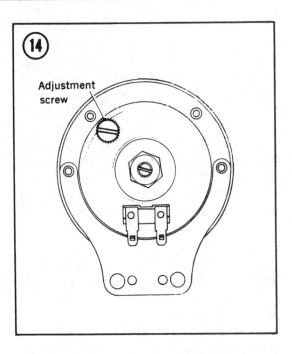

Turn Signals

If any turn signal bulb burns out, be sure to replace it with the same type. Improper action of the flasher relay, or even failure to operate may result from use of the wrong bulbs.

Brake Lights

The brake light switch is actuated by the brake pedal. Adjust the switch so that the stoplight goes on just before braking action occurs. Move the switch body as required for adjustment. Tighten the clamp nut after adjustment.

HORN

Current for the horn is supplied by the battery. One horn terminal is connected to the battery through the main switch. The other terminal is connected to the horn button. When the rider presses the button, current flows through the horn.

Figure 14 illustrates horn construction. As current flows through the coil, the core becomes magnetized and attracts the armature. As the armature moves, it opens the contacts, cutting off the current. The diaphragm spring then returns the armature to its original position. This process repeats rapidly until the rider releases the horn button. Action of the armature striking the end of the core produces the sound, which is amplified by the resonator.

MAIN SWITCH

Service of the main switch is limited to checking continuity between the various circuits.

BATTERY

Most Yamaha bikes are equipped with lead-acid storage batteries, smaller in size but similar in construction to those found in automobiles.

WARNING
Read and thoroughly understand the section on safety precautions before doing any battery service.

Safety Precautions

When working with batteries, use extreme care to avoid spilling or splashing electrolyte.

This electrolyte is sulphuric acid, which can destroy clothing and cause serious chemical burns. If any electrolyte is spilled or splashed on clothing or body, it should immediately be neutralized with a solution of baking soda and water, then flushed with plenty of clean water.

Electrolyte splashed into the eyes is extremely dangerous. Safety glasses should always be worn when working with batteries. If electrolyte is splashed into the eye, force the eye open, flood with cool clean water for about 5 minutes, and call a physician immediately.

If electrolyte is spilled or splashed onto painted or unpainted surfaces, it should be neutralized immediately with baking soda solution and then rinsed with clean water.

When batteries are being charged, highly explosive hydrogen gas forms in each cell. Some of this gas escapes through the filler openings and may form an explosive atmosphere around the battery. *This explosive atmosphere may exist for hours.* Sparks, open flame, or a lighted cigarette can ignite this gas, causing an internal explosion and possible serious personal injury. The following precautions should be taken to prevent an explosion.

1. Do not smoke or permit any open flame near any battery being charged or which has been recently charged.

2. Do not disconnect live circuits at battery terminals, because a spark usually occurs where a live circuit is broken. Care must always be taken when connecting or disconnecting any battery charger; be sure its power switch is off before making or breaking connections. Poor connections are a common cause of electrical arcs which cause explosions.

Electrolyte Level

Battery electrolyte level should be checked regularly, particularly during hot weather. Most batteries are marked with electrolyte level limit lines (**Figure 15**). Always maintain the fluid level between these lines, using distilled water as required for replenishment. Distilled water is

available at most supermarkets. It is sold for use in steam irons and is quite inexpensive.

Overfilling leads to loss of electrolyte, resulting in poor battery performance, short life, and excessive corrosion. Never allow the electrolyte level to drop below the top of the plates. That portion of the plates exposed to air may be permanently damaged, resulting in loss of battery performance and shortened life.

Excessive use of water is an indication that the battery is being overcharged. The most common causes of overcharging are high battery temperature or high voltage regulator setting.

Cleaning

Check the battery occasionally for presence of dirt or corrosion. The top of the battery, in particular, should be kept clean. Acid film and dirt permit current to flow between terminals, which will slowly discharge the battery.

For best results when cleaning, wash first with diluted ammonia or baking soda solution, then flush with plenty of clean water. Take care to keep filler plugs tight so that no cleaning solution enters the cells.

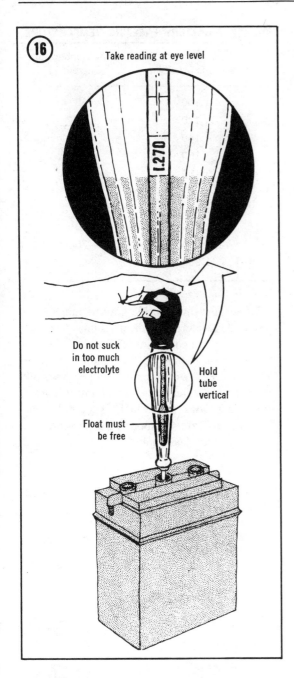

(16)

Take reading at eye level

1.270

Hold tube vertical

Do not suck in too much electrolyte

Float must be free

Battery Cables

To ensure good electrical contact, cables must be clean and tight on battery terminals. If the battery or cable terminals are corroded, the cables should be disconnected and cleaned separately with a wire brush and baking soda solution. After cleaning, apply a very thin coating of petroleum jelly to the battery terminals before installing the cables. After connecting the cables, apply a light coating to the connection. This procedure will help to prevent future corrosion.

Battery Charging

WARNING
Do not smoke or permit any open flame in any area where batteries are being charged, or immediately after charging. Highly explosive hydrogen gas is formed during the charging process. Be sure to reread Safety Precautions *in the beginning of this section.*

Motorcycle batteries are not designed for high charge or discharge rates. For this reason, it is recommended that a motorcycle battery be charged at a rate not exceeding 10 percent of its ampere-hour capacity. That is, do not exceed 0.5 ampere charging rate for a 5 ampere-hour battery. This charge rate should continue for 10 hours if the battery is completely discharged, or until specific gravity of each cell is up to 1.260-1.280, corrected for temperature. If after prolonged charging, specific gravity of one or more cells does not come up to at least 1.230, the battery will not perform as well as it should, but it may continue to provide satisfactory service for a time.

Some temperature rise is normal as a battery is being charged. Do not allow the electrolyte temperature to exceed 110°F. Should temperature reach that figure, discontinue charging until the battery cools, then resume charging at a lower rate.

Testing State of Charge

Although sophisticated battery testing devices are on the market, they are not available to the average motorcycle owner, and their use is beyond the scope of this book. A hydrometer, however, is an inexpensive tool, and will tell much about battery condition.

To use a hydrometer, place the suction tube into the filler opening and draw in just enough electrolyte to lift the float. Hold the instrument in a vertical position and read specific gravity on the scale, where the float stem emerges from the electrolyte (**Figure 16**).

6

Table 6   STATE OF CHARGE

Specific Gravity	State of Charge
1.110-1.130	Discharged
1.140-1.160	Almost discharged
1.170-1.190	One-quarter charged
1.200-1.220	One-half charged
1.230-1.250	Three-quarters charged
1.260-1.280	Fully charged

Table 7   BATTERY FREEZING TEMPERATURE

Specific Gravity	Freezing Temperature (Degrees F)
1.100	18
1.120	13
1.140	8
1.160	1
1.180	—6
1.200	—17
1.220	—31
1.240	—50
1.260	—75
1.280	—92

Specific gravity of the electrolyte varies with temperature, so it is necessary to apply a temperature correction to the reading so obtained. For each 10 degrees that battery temperature exceeds 80°F, add 0.004 to the indicated specific gravity. Likewise, subtract 0.004 from the indicated value for each 10 degrees that battery temperature is below 80°F.

Repeat this measurement for each battery cell. If there is more than 0.050 difference (50 points) between cells, battery condition is questionable.

State of charge may be determined from **Table 6**.

Do not measure specific gravity immediately after adding water. Ride the machine a few miles to ensure thorough mixing of the electrolyte.

It is most important to maintain batteries fully charged during cold weather. A fully charged battery freezes at a much lower temperature than does one which is partially discharged. Freezing temperature depends on specific gravity. See **Table 7**.

CHAPTER SEVEN

CHASSIS SERVICE

This chapter discusses service operations on wheels, brakes, suspension components, and related items. Chassis service is generally similar for all models; differences are pointed out where they exist.

WHEELS

Except for removal and installation, service on front and rear wheels is generally similar; differences are pointed out where they exist.

Front Wheel Removal/Installation

Figure 1 is an exploded view of a typical front wheel. Refer to that illustration during front wheel removal and service.

1. Support motorcycle so that front wheel is clear of ground. A box placed under the engine is a suitable support.

2. Disconnect brake cable at front brake lever (**Figure 2**).

3. Disconnect brake cable and speedometer cable at front wheel hub.

4. Loosen front axle pinch bolt (**Figure 3**) and cap bolts at lower end of the forks, if so equipped.

5. Remove axle nut (**Figure 4**).

6. Insert shank of a Phillips screwdriver into hole in axle, then simultaneously twist and pull the axle to remove it.

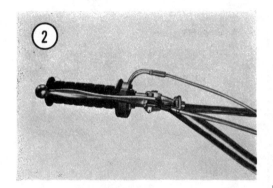

7. Roll wheel away from motorcycle. Be sure to catch any small parts, such as spacers, if they fall.

8. Front wheel installation is the reverse of removal. Be sure to tighten the axle pinch bolts and adjust the front brake.

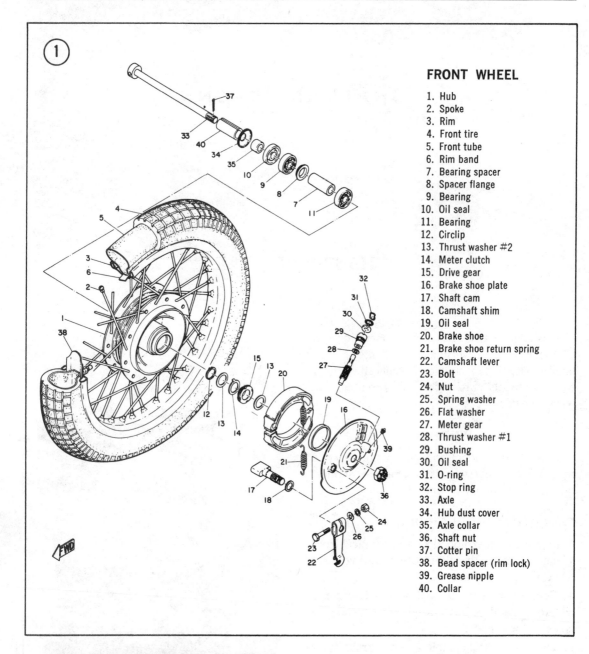

①

FRONT WHEEL

1. Hub
2. Spoke
3. Rim
4. Front tire
5. Front tube
6. Rim band
7. Bearing spacer
8. Spacer flange
9. Bearing
10. Oil seal
11. Bearing
12. Circlip
13. Thrust washer #2
14. Meter clutch
15. Drive gear
16. Brake shoe plate
17. Shaft cam
18. Camshaft shim
19. Oil seal
20. Brake shoe
21. Brake shoe return spring
22. Camshaft lever
23. Bolt
24. Nut
25. Spring washer
26. Flat washer
27. Meter gear
28. Thrust washer #1
29. Bushing
30. Oil seal
31. O-ring
32. Stop ring
33. Axle
34. Hub dust cover
35. Axle collar
36. Shaft nut
37. Cotter pin
38. Bead spacer (rim lock)
39. Grease nipple
40. Collar

④

Rear Wheel Removal/Installation

Figures 5 and 6 are exploded views of typical rear wheels. Some models are equipped with rubber dampers in the rear hubs.

1. Support motorcycle so that rear wheel is clear of ground.

2. Remove brake rod and brake torque link from rear brake.

3. Loosen drive chain adjustment nuts on each side.

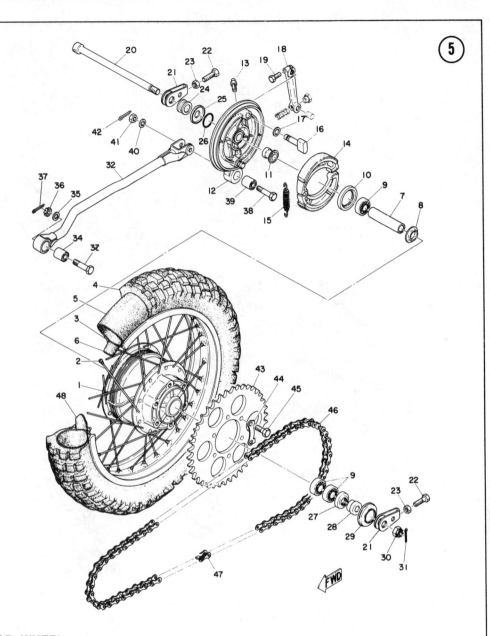

REAR WHEEL

1. Rear hub	13. Grease nipple	25. Dust cover plate	37. Cotter pin
2. Spoke	14. Brake shoe	26. O-ring	38. Bolt
3. Rim	15. Return spring	27. Grease seal	39. Bushing
4. Tire	16. Brake actuating camshaft	28. Axle collar	40. Lockwasher
5. Tube	17. Camshaft shim	29. Dust cover plate	41. Nut
6. Rim band	18. Camshaft lever	30. Axle nut	42. Cotter pin
7. Bearing spacer	19. Bolt	31. Cotter pin	43. Sprocket
8. Spacer flange	20. Axle	32. Tension bar	44. Lockwasher
9. Bearing	21. Chain adjuster	33. Bolt	45. Bolt
10. Grease seal	22. Chain adjuster bolt	34. Bushing	46. Chain
11. Shaft bushing	23. Nut	35. Lockwasher	47. Chain master link
12. Brake shoe plate	24. Axle spacer	36. Slotted nut	48. Rim lock

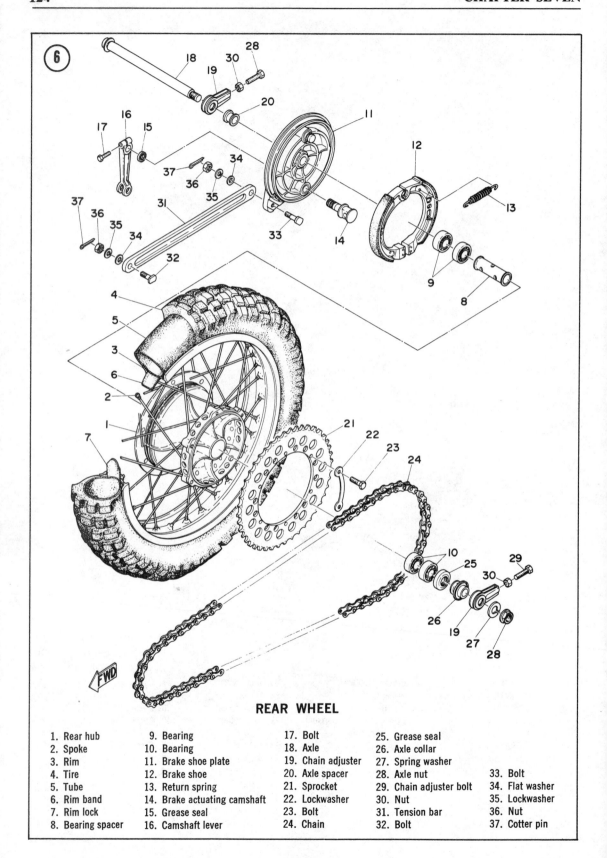

REAR WHEEL

1. Rear hub	9. Bearing	17. Bolt	25. Grease seal
2. Spoke	10. Bearing	18. Axle	26. Axle collar
3. Rim	11. Brake shoe plate	19. Chain adjuster	27. Spring washer
4. Tire	12. Brake shoe	20. Axle spacer	28. Axle nut
5. Tube	13. Return spring	21. Sprocket	29. Chain adjuster bolt	33. Bolt
6. Rim band	14. Brake actuating camshaft	22. Lockwasher	30. Nut	34. Flat washer
7. Rim lock	15. Grease seal	23. Bolt	31. Tension bar	35. Lockwasher
8. Bearing spacer	16. Camshaft lever	24. Chain	32. Bolt	36. Nut
				37. Cotter pin

4. Remove rear axle nut.

5. Drive out rear axle, using a rawhide or plastic mallet.

6. Remove right-hand chain adjuster.

7. Remove rear brake plate.

8. Tilt motorcycle to the left, then roll rear wheel free.

9. Reverse the removal procedure to install the rear wheel. Be sure that all fasteners are tight, that the drive chain is adjusted, and that the rear brake is adjusted properly.

Spokes

Check spokes for tension. The "tuning fork" method for checking tension is simple and works well. Tap each spoke with a spoke wrench or screwdriver shank. A taut spoke will emit a clear, ringing tone; a loose spoke will sound flat. All spokes in a correctly tightened wheel will emit tones of similar pitch, but not necessarily the same tone.

Bent, stripped, or otherwise damaged spokes should be replaced as soon as they are detected. Unscrew the nipple from the spoke, then push the nipple far enough into the rim to free the end of the spoke, taking care not to push the spoke all the way in. Remove the defective spoke from the hub, then use it to match a new one of the same length. If necessary, trim the end of the new spoke slightly to match the original, then dress the threads. Install the new spoke, screw on the nipple, and tighten it until it emits a tone similar to that of the other spokes when it is struck. Check the new spoke periodically; it will stretch and so must be retightened several times until it takes its final set.

Spokes tend to loosen as the machine is used. Retighten each spoke one turn, beginning with those on one side of the hub, then those on the other side. Tighten the spokes on a new machine after the first 50 miles of operation, then at 50-mile intervals until they no longer loosen.

If the machine is subjected to off-road or competition riding, check the spokes frequently.

Bead Protectors

Some machines are equipped with a bead protector (**Figure 7**) on each wheel. The bead

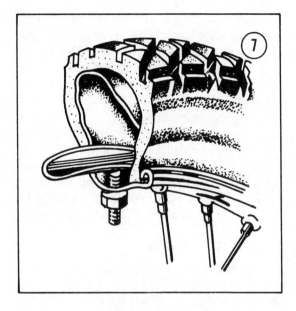

protector prevents the tire from slipping on the rim, especially during maximum effort braking at high speed, and thereby prevents damage to the valve stem.

Rims

Check rims periodically for runout and out-of-round; also for bends or dents following a collision or a hard spill. Severe rim damage is difficult to repair successfully, and it is generally wise and safer to replace the rim in such cases. The rubber rim band, which covers the spoke nipples and prevents them from chafing the inner tube, should be checked carefully each time the tire is removed. If the rim band is torn, exposing a spoke, replace or repair it with tape.

Wheel Balance

An unbalanced wheel results in unsafe riding conditions. Depending on the degree of un-balance and speed of the motorcycle, the rider may experience anything from a mild vibration to a violent shimmy which may even result in loss of control. Balance weights may be installed on spokes on the light side of the wheel to correct this condition.

Before attempting to balance wheels, check to be sure that the wheel bearings are in good condition and properly lubricated. Also make sure that brakes do not drag, so that wheels rotate freely. With the wheel free of the ground, spin

7

it slowly and allow it to come to rest by itself. Add balance weights to the spokes on the light side as required, so that the wheel comes to rest at a different position each time it is spun. Balance weights are available in weights of 10, 20, and 30 grams. Remove the drive chain before balancing rear wheels.

If more than one ounce is required to balance the wheel, add weight to adjacent spokes; never put 2 or more weights on the same spoke. When the wheel comes to rest at a different point each time it is spun, consider it balanced and tightly crimp the weights so they will not be thrown off.

Checking Wheel Runout

To measure runout of the wheel rim, support the wheel so it is free to rotate. Position a dial indicator as shown in **Figure 8**. Observe the dial indicator as you rotate the wheel through a complete revolution. The runout limit for all models is 0.07 in. (2.0mm). Excessive runout may be caused by a bent rim or loose spokes. Repair or replace as required.

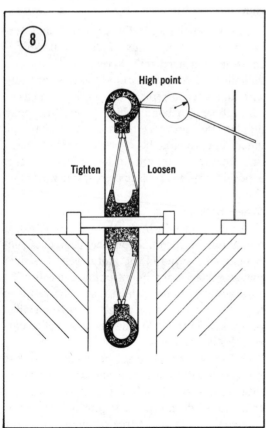

High point

Tighten　　　Loosen

Miscellaneous Wheel Checks

1. Support each wheel shaft in a lathe, V-blocks, or other suitable centering device as shown in **Figure 9**. Rotate the shaft through a complete revolution. Straighten or replace the shaft if it is bent more than 0.028 in. (0.7mm).

2. Check the inner and outer races of the wheel bearings for cracks, galling, or pitting. Rotate the bearings by hand and check for roughness. Replace the bearings if they are worn or damaged.

3. Inspect oil seals for wear or damage. Replace them if there is any doubt about their condition.

Front Wheel Bearing
Removal/Installation

1. Clean dirt from wheel hub.

2. Make a bearing spacer removal tool, similar to that shown in **Figure 10**.

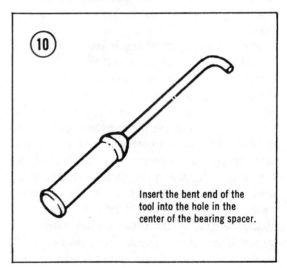

Insert the bent end of the tool into the hole in the center of the bearing spacer.

3. Refer to **Figure 11**. Place the bent end of the tool into the hole in the bearing spacer, then drive out the spacer and one bearing.

4. Drive out the remaining bearing.

5. Reverse the removal procedure to install the front wheel bearings. Always clean and relubricate them whenever they are removed.

> **CAUTION**
> *Be sure to install the spacer flange, on models so equipped. Failure to do so will result in premature bearing failure.*

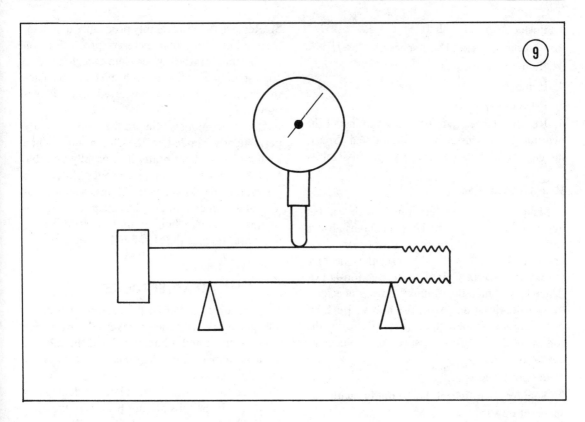

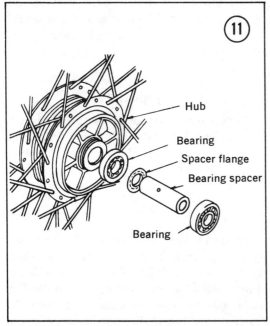

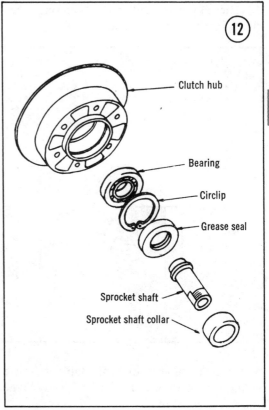

Clutch Hub Replacement

Figure 12 is an exploded view of a typical clutch hub on models with rear hub cushions. To replace bearings in such hubs:

1. Push out sprocket shaft.

2. Pull out sprocket shaft spacer.

3. Remove grease seal.

4. Remove snap ring.

5. Press out bearing.

6. Reverse the removal procedure to install the bearing. Always install a new grease seal. Grease the bearing and grease seal lips upon assembly.

Rear Hub Cushions

Some models are equipped with rubber cushions in the rear hub. These cushions absorb sudden torque loads in the transmission, drive chain, and rear wheel. With use, they become worn and broken. Complete destruction is evidenced by a metallic "clunk" during acceleration or deceleration. Also, the hub will exhibit considerable angular free play. Perform the following procedure to inspect or replace the cushions.

1. Remove rear wheel.

2. Support rear wheel horizontally, with the sprocket upward.

3. Refer to **Figure 13**. Remove snap rings, then clutch hub to expose cushions.

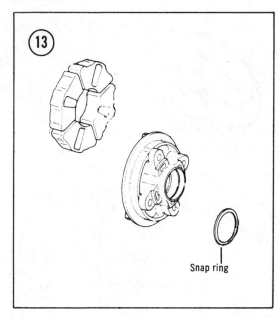

Snap ring

4. Inspect cushion cavities and snap ring groove in hub for cracks or other damage. Replace the hub in the event of damage.

5. Reverse the disassembly procedure to assemble the hub. Note that there are protrusions on the bottom of the clutch hub which fit into corresponding holes in each cushion. Replace the snap ring if it was distorted when it was removed.

On some models, the rubber cushions are permanently bonded to the clutch hub. When such cushions deteriorate, it is usually possible to tighten them and restore proper clutch hub operation. To do so, place shims, available at Yamaha dealers, under the snap ring which retains the clutch hub. If that procedure does not work, replace the clutch hub.

REAR SPROCKET

To remove the sprocket, place the wheel on a level surface with the sprocket upward. Using a blunt punch and a hammer, bend the tabs on the locking plate flat. Then remove the sprocket mounting bolts.

Check the bolts and lock plate for damage or breakage. If the tabs are not bent over the bolt, or are broken, or if the bolts are loose, the sprocket will loosen. Torque sprocket mounting bolts to 15 ft.-lb. (2.0 mkg). Be sure that all lock tabs are tight.

BRAKES

Each brake consists of a brake pedal or lever, cable or rod, brake shoe plate, and drum. The brake shoe plate assembly includes the brake cam, lever, brake shoes, retracting springs, and plate.

Operation

Figure 14 illustrates typical brake operation. When the camshaft turns, it forces both shoes against the brake drum. Movement of the brake drum tends to increase the pressure of the forward shoe against the drum, therefore the forward shoe is a leading shoe because of this self-energizing effect. The rear shoe, however, makes contact in the direction of the drum rotation, and the self-energizing effect does not occur. Therefore, the rear brake shoe is a trailing shoe.

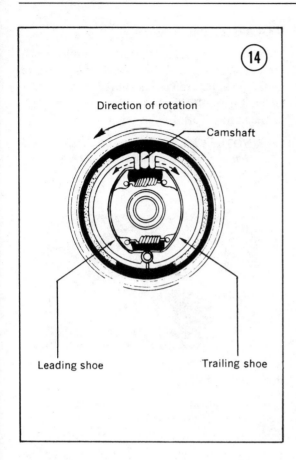

Direction of rotation

Camshaft

Leading shoe   Trailing shoe

Table 1   BRAKE WEAR LIMITS

Model	Standard size		Wear limit	
	Inches	Millimeters	Inches	Millimeters
250	5.91	150	5.71	145
YZ250	6.30	160	6.22	158
360	5.91	150	5.71	145
YZ360	6.30	160	6.22	158
400	6.30	160	6.22	158

Inspection

Measure outer diameter of the brake shoe assembly, as shown in **Figure 15**. Wear limits for the various models are listed in **Table 1**.

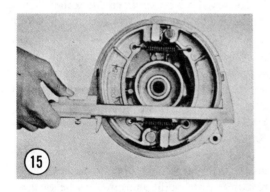

Examine inner surfaces of the brake drums for cracks, grooves, or other damage. Any groove deep enough to catch a fingernail is cause to consider brake drum replacement.

Replace any brake shoes that are oil soaked immediately.

Replacing Brake Shoes

Place the brake shoe plate on a firm, flat surfaces, with the brake shoes upward, then proceed as follows.

1. Hold one shoe securely, then carefully lift the other shoe until it pivots away from the anchor and pivot at its ends. Be careful; the return springs are under considerable tension.

2. Unhook both return springs.

3. Remove remaining shoe.

4. Place both new shoes on a flat surface, then install both return springs.

5. Place one shoe in position, with its flat end against the brake cam, and its radiused end against the stationary anchor pin.

6. Hold the shoe installed in Step 5, then slip the ends of the remaining shoe over the anchor pin and cam. Finally, press the shoe into position against the brake shoe plate (**Figure 16**).

7

7. Turn the cam slightly, and apply grease sparingly to the contact surfaces shown in **Figure 17**.

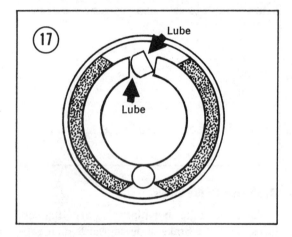

Front Brake Adjustment

Refer to **Figure 18**. Loosen locknut (A), then turn cable adjuster (B) to provide 0.2-0.3 in. (5-8mm) clearance to the mounting bracket when all cable slack is taken up.

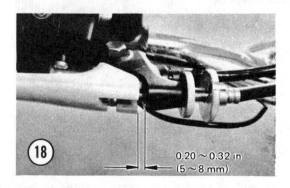

Some models are equipped with an additional adjuster at the front wheel. Use it as needed.

Rear Brake Adjustment

Proper rear brake adjustment results when there is approximately one inch (25mm) brake pedal travel before the rear brake starts to take effect. **Figure 19** illustrates the rear brake adjustment nut. Turn it in or out as required.

> NOTE: *There is no locknut. Be sure that the special spring is in place on the rod, just forward of the rear brake lever.*

Rear Brake Modification

Rear brake action may be too sensive for some riders. If the rear wheel locks, and skidding results, try the following procedure.

1. Bend the rod which connect the brake pedal and rear brake lever until it has a definite and permanent bow. This procedure is usually enough to decrease rear brake sensitivity, but if not, continue with Step 2.

2. Remove both brake shoes. Mark them so that they may be returned to their original locations.

3. Carefully clamp each brake shoe in a vise, then file grooves at an angle across the friction surfaces (**Figure 20**). These grooves should be approximately ¼ in. (6mm) wide, and no deeper than ½ the thickness of the lining. Slightly chamfer the edge of the grooves which contact the brake drum.

To start, space the grooves about 2 in. (5 cm) apart, then reassemble the brake and test its response. Add additional grooves between the original ones if necessary.

FRONT FORKS

All models are equipped with oil-damped telescopic front forks. **Figures 21 and 22** are exploded views of typical forks on these models.

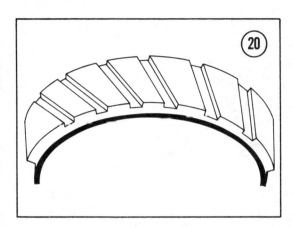

Refer to the applicable illustration during fork removal and service.

Fork Removal

Fork removal is generally similar for all models.

1. Support front of motorcycle so that front wheel is clear of ground.

2. Remove front wheel.

3. Remove front fender and fork brace.

4. Remove tachometer and speedometer, if so equipped.

5. Refer to **Figure 23**. Loosen pinch bolts (A), then remove fork cap bolts (B).

> **WARNING**
> *This cap bolt is under considerable spring pressure. Hold it to prevent it from flying off and causing possible injury.*

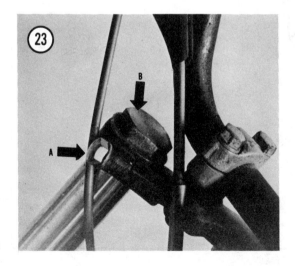

> **WARNING**
> *On models with air forks, release pressure from low pressure valve (**Figure 24**) before removing air chamber.*

6. Remove air chambers on models so equipped (**Figure 25**).

7. Refer to **Figure 26**. Loosen pinch bolts (C).

8. Support headlight assembly, if so equipped, then pull fork tube downward to remove it from steering head.

132

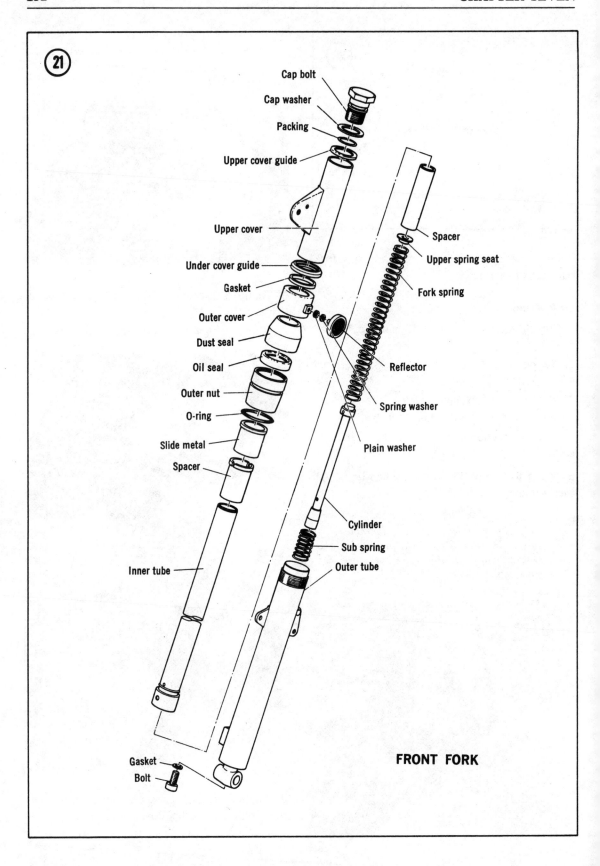

(21)

Cap bolt

Cap washer

Packing

Upper cover guide

Upper cover

Spacer

Upper spring seat

Under cover guide

Gasket

Fork spring

Outer cover

Dust seal

Oil seal

Reflector

Outer nut

O-ring

Spring washer

Slide metal

Plain washer

Spacer

Inner tube

Cylinder

Sub spring

Outer tube

Gasket

Bolt

FRONT FORK

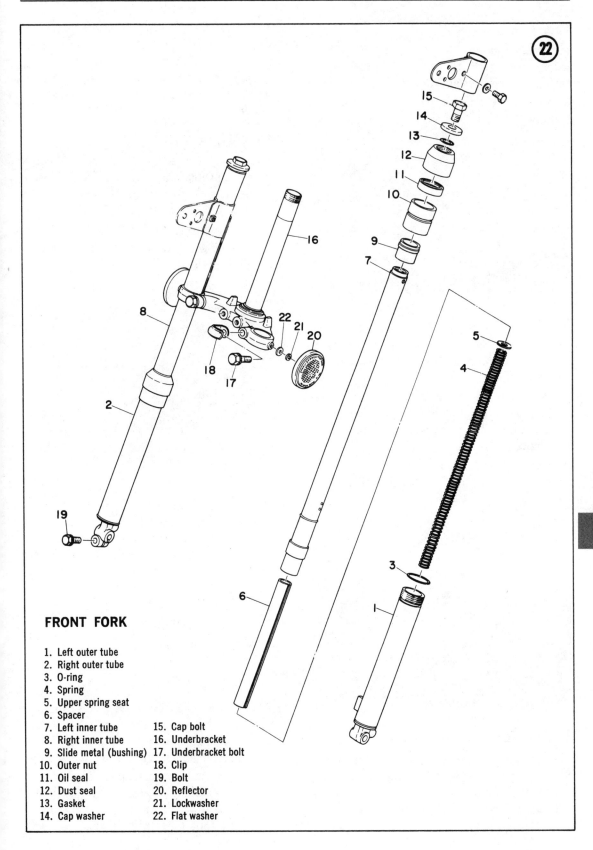

FRONT FORK

1. Left outer tube
2. Right outer tube
3. O-ring
4. Spring
5. Upper spring seat
6. Spacer
7. Left inner tube
8. Right inner tube
9. Slide metal (bushing)
10. Outer nut
11. Oil seal
12. Dust seal
13. Gasket
14. Cap washer
15. Cap bolt
16. Underbracket
17. Underbracket bolt
18. Clip
19. Bolt
20. Reflector
21. Lockwasher
22. Flat washer

Fork Tube Disassembly

1. Obtain a suitable drain pan, then invert fork leg to drain its oil. Note that the spacer, upper spring seat, and spring will fall out at this time.
2. Remove Allen bolt from outer fork tube (**Figure 27**).

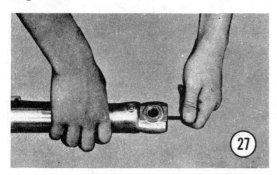

3. Refer back to Figure 21. On models with an outer nut (left center of illustration), continue with Step 4. On models without this nut, pull fork tubes apart.
4. Wrap a piece of old inner tube or similar rubber sheet around outer tube nut, then clamp it in a vise. Turn outer tube counterclockwise to remove nut and separate tubes.
5. Remove damper unit (**Figure 28**). On some models, the damper unit is retained by a snap ring, which must be removed first.

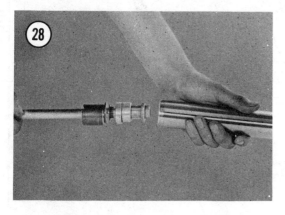

Fork Inspection

Check inner fork tubes for bends or scratches. Slightly bent tubes may be straightened. Any rust or corrosion on the inner fork tube in the area where it passes through the oil seal is cause for replacement.

Compare overall spring length with that of new springs. If they are shorter than new ones by ¼ in. (6mm), replace both springs.

Seepage past the oil seal indicates need for oil seal replacement.

Oil Seal Replacement

On models with a ring nut which holds both fork tubes together, the oil seal is located inside the ring nut; on other models, the oil seal is located inside the outer tube.

1. Pry out snap ring washer and dust seal.
2. Refer to **Figure 29**. Carefully pry out oil seal, using a folded rag to protect the outer tube.

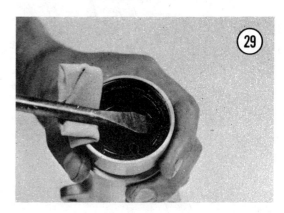

3. Position new seal with its open end downward, then gently tap all around its exposed surface to start it into position. Once it is started, use a socket wrench of appropriate diameter as a seal driver and a light hammer to seat it.
4. Install dust seal, washer, and snap ring.
5. Lubricate oil seal lip.
6. Assemble fork leg.

Fork Assembly

1. To assemble the front fork, reverse the disassembly procedure. Be sure that the inner tube slides in and out smoothly. Always replace the oil seal under the outer tube nut upon assembly.
2. To install the front fork on the frame, place each tube assembly in the correct position. Tighten both lower pinch bolts just enough to prevent the fork tube from falling, then add

fork oil. Install and tighten the cap bolt completely. Then tighten both lower and upper pinch bolts.

3. On models with air forks, tighten air chambers to 18-25 ft.-lb. (2.5-3.5 mkg), then safety-wire them into position (**Figure 30**). Pressurize low pressure chambers to 24-35 psi and high pressure chambers to 51-70 psi.

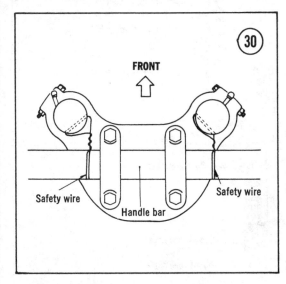

NOTE: *Refill each fork leg with 10W-30 motor oil through the opening in the upper end. The correct oil quantity is listed in* **Table 2**.

Table 2   FORK OIL QUANTITY

Model	Oil Quantity	
	Ounces	Milliliters
DT1, -B, -C	7.1	210
DT1-E, DT1E-MX	5.9	175
DT2, -MX	5.9	175
DT3, MX250, DT250	5.9	175
MX250A, YZ250	6.6	195
RT1, -MX	7.1	210
RT1B, -MX	5.9	175
RT2, -MX	5.9	175
RT3	5.9	175
MX360	5.9	175
YZ360	6.6	195
YZ400	14.1	415
DT400	5.9	175
SC500 series	6.6	195

Fork Oil Change

Water, dust, and aluminum particles gradually contaminate the fork oil. For this reason, fork oil should be changed every 4,000 miles (6,500 kilometers) on models used for street riding, and much more frequently on those models used for off-road riding.

1. Place a suitable collection vessel under each fork leg.

2. Remove fork oil drain screws (**Figure 31**).

3. Lock front brake, then pump forks up and down until all oil drains.

4. Replace drain screws. Be careful; it is easy to cross-thread these screws.

5. Loosen upper pinch bolts (A, Figure 23), then remove fork cap bolts.

WARNING
Fork cap bolts are under considerable spring pressure. Hold them firmly to prevent them from flying away and causing possible injury.

6. Fill each fork leg with the correct amount of fork oil specified in foregoing Table 2.

7. Lock front brake, then pump forks up and down gently until all oil has drained into the lower portion of each fork leg.

8. Install fork cap bolts, then tighten upper pinch bolts.

STEERING HEAD

Figures 32 and 33 are exploded views of typical steering heads. Refer to the appropriate illustration during steering head disassembly and service.

7

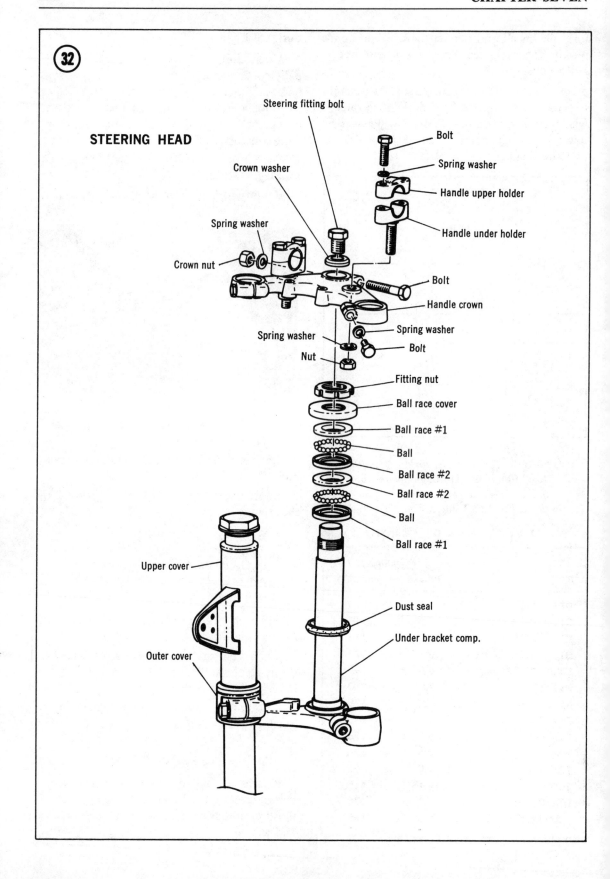

STEERING HEAD

- Steering fitting bolt
- Crown washer
- Spring washer
- Crown nut
- Bolt
- Spring washer
- Handle upper holder
- Handle under holder
- Bolt
- Handle crown
- Spring washer
- Spring washer
- Bolt
- Nut
- Fitting nut
- Ball race cover
- Ball race #1
- Ball
- Ball race #2
- Ball race #2
- Ball
- Ball race #1
- Upper cover
- Outer cover
- Dust seal
- Under bracket comp.

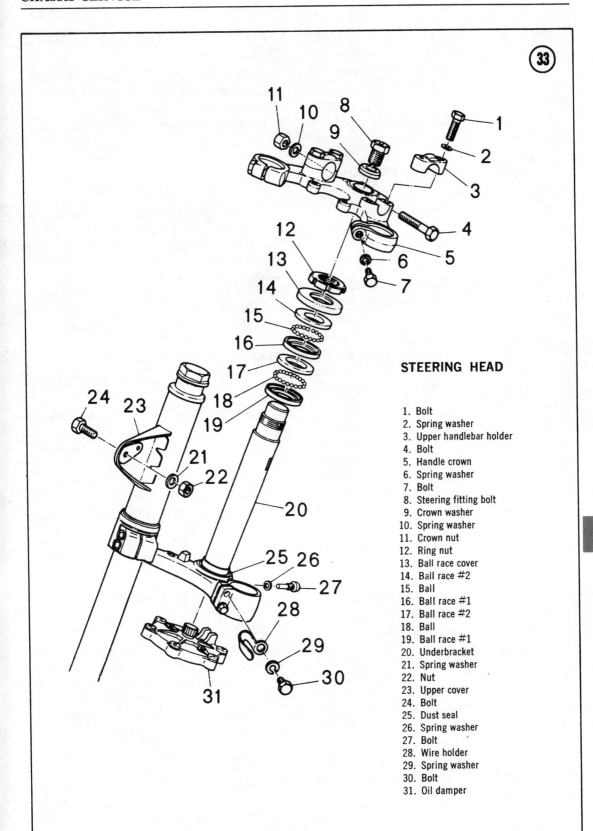

33

STEERING HEAD

1. Bolt
2. Spring washer
3. Upper handlebar holder
4. Bolt
5. Handle crown
6. Spring washer
7. Bolt
8. Steering fitting bolt
9. Crown washer
10. Spring washer
11. Crown nut
12. Ring nut
13. Ball race cover
14. Ball race #2
15. Ball
16. Ball race #1
17. Ball race #2
18. Ball
19. Ball race #1
20. Underbracket
21. Spring washer
22. Nut
23. Upper cover
24. Bolt
25. Dust seal
26. Spring washer
27. Bolt
28. Wire holder
29. Spring washer
30. Bolt
31. Oil damper

7

Check steering head bearing races and balls occasionally for pitting, cracks, or wear. If any of these conditions exist, replace all balls and races. Never use any combination of new and used parts.

1. Disconnect clutch cable, throttle cable, and front brake cable at handlebar.

2. Remove headlight, if so equipped, and disconnect any wiring to switches on handlebar.

3. Remove handlebar.

4. Remove speedometer and tachometer, if so equipped.

5. Remove front wheel.

6. Remove both front fork legs.

7. Remove steering damper, if so equipped.

8. Remove bolt from center of upper bracket, then remove upper bracket.

9. Remove ring nut (12, Figure 33). This nut may be started by tapping it counterclockwise with a small hammer and punch. Hold lower bracket to prevent it from dropping and balls from falling out.

10. Remove race cover, upper race, and all upper balls. Note that there are 22 small balls in the upper bearing. A small magnet may be helpful during this step.

11. Lower underbracket slighlty, then remove 19 lower balls. Hold a rag under the work area to catch any balls that may drop.

12. Tap out inner races, if necessary, with a long drift and small hammer.

13. To remove the lowermost race, carefully wedge it up over the underbracket stem.

Steering head assembly is the reverse of disassembly. Observe the following notes.

1. Tap races in carefully until they are fully seated.

2. Apply heavy grease to the lowermost race (on underbracket stem) to hold balls in position, then install all 19 balls. Apply more grease after balls are in position.

3. Hold underbracket in position, grease upper bearing race liberally, install 22 small balls, then apply more grease.

4. Complete assembly in reverse order of disassembly.

To adjust steering head bearing, proceed as follows.

1. Using a hammer and suitable drift, tighten ring nut until fork turns from one limit to the other with no binding or looseness.

2. Install all remaining parts, then again check the adjustment.

REAR SUSPENSION

On most models, the rear suspension consists of a swinging arm assembly, 3-position adjustable springs, and shock absorbers. On some models, a single Monocross shock absorber is combined with a swinging arm. **Figure 34** is an exploded view of a typical rear suspension system with dual shock absorbers. **Figure 35** illustrates Yamaha's Monocross suspension.

Shock Absorbers

To check shock absorbers, remove one of them from the motorcycle by unbolting its retaining hardware. Leave the remaining unit in place.

> NOTE: *Comparing resistance of an old shock with a new one is not a valid test. New seals will make the new shock appear to have far greater dampening than it actually does.*

1. Press upper end of spring downward, remove both half-moon keepers, then remove spring.

2. Extend shock absorber shaft fully.

3. Push shaft in quickly. It should go in with little resistance.

4. Push shaft in fully.

5. Try to pull shaft out quickly. The shock absorber shaft must slide out slowly, no matter how hard it is pulled. Replace the shock absorber if the shaft pulls out easily.

6. Assemble spring and shock absorber, then install assembly on motorcycle.

7. Remove remaining shock absorber, then repeat Steps 1 through 6.

On models with Thermal Flow shock absorbers, it is possible to change shock absorber fluid when it becomes contaminated, or to alter suspension damping characteristics.

REAR SUSPENSION

1. Swinging arm
2. Bushing
3. Bushing
4. Shim
5. Cover
6. Pivot shaft
7. Washer
8. Nut
9. Grease fitting
10. Shock absorber
11. Spring seat
12. Bolt
13. Chaincase
14. Grommet
15. Spacer
16. Washer
17. Screw
18. Chain guard
19. Bolt
20. Washer
21. Washer
22. Bolt
23. Washer
24. Seal

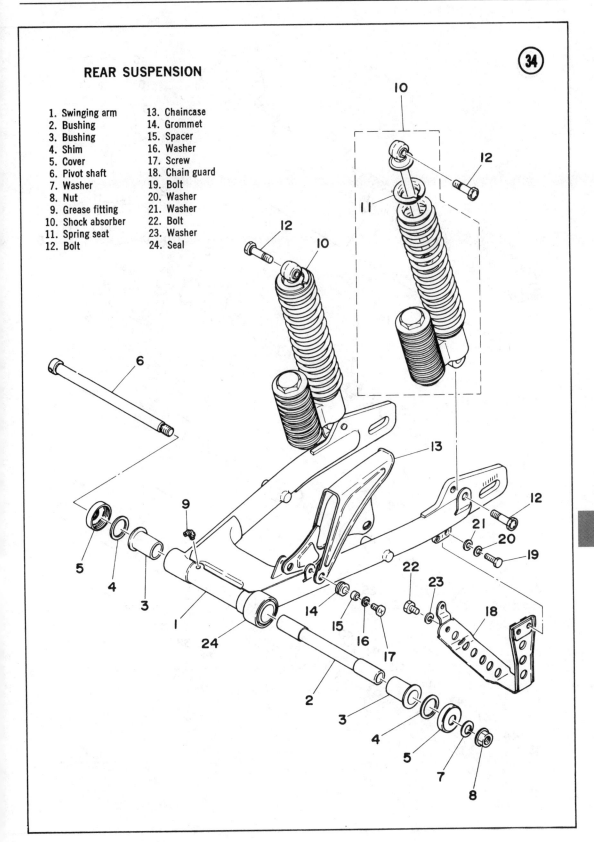

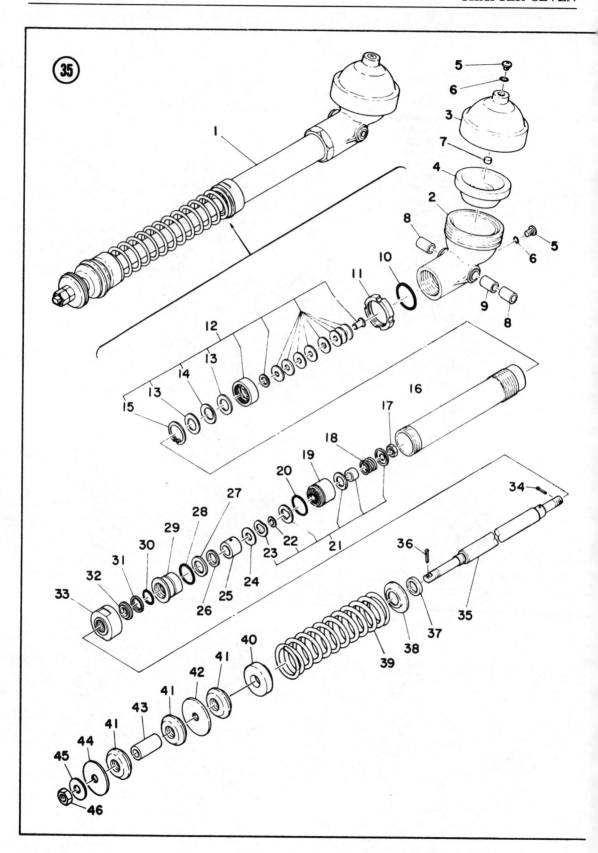

MONOCROSS REAR SUSPENSION

1. Monocross assembly
2. Diaphragm housing
3. Cap
4. Diaphragm
5. Screw
6. O-ring
7. Valve
8. Bushing
9. Spacer
10. O-ring
11. Ring nut
12. Base valve set
13. Plate
14. Spring
15. Snap ring
16. Cylinder
17. Nut
18. Spring
19. Piston
20. O-ring
21. Piston valve set
22. Plate
23. Spring
24. Washer
25. Stopper
26. Spacer
27. Damper
28. O-ring
29. Seal ring housing
30. O-ring
31. O-ring
32. Oil seal
33. Cap
34. Cotter pin
35. Piston rod
36. Cotter pin
37. Washer
38. Spring guide
39. Spring
40. Spring seat
41. Damper
42. Nut plate
43. Spacer
44. Washer
45. Washer
46. Nut

1. Remove reservoir cap, then pour out and discard existing fluid.

2. Slowly pump plunger to expel remaining fluid.

3. Pour in 6.0 ounces (175cc) shock fluid into reservoir.

4. Slowly pump plunger to bleed out entrapped air.

5. Install reservoir cap, then tighten it to 36-43 ft.-lb. (5.0-6.0 mkg).

Monocross Suspension Unit

WARNING
Monocross shock absorbers contain nitrogen gas under high pressure. Use only nitrogen when refilling the suspension unit.
Do not attempt to disassemble the suspension unit.
Do not incinerate discarded Monocross suspension units.

To replace the Monocross unit:

1. Turn fuel petcock off, then remove fuel tank.

2. Remove both pivot shaft nuts. Upon installation, tighten these nuts to 51 ft.-lb. (9.0 mkg). Remove washer and bushing.

3. Remove bolt which secures diaphragm housing to rear of frame. Take care not to lose its washer. Upon installation, tighten nut to 14.5 ft.-lb. (2.0 mkg).

4. Lift swinging arm, then pull out suspension unit from rear.

5. Reverse the removal procedure to install the suspension unit.

A few items on the Monocross suspension system require periodic inspection. Refer to **Figure 36**.

1. Remove spring.

2. Loosen ring nut (2).

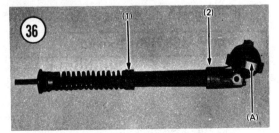

36 (1) (2) (A)

3. Tighten case cap (1) to 108 ft.-lb. (15 mkg).

4. Retighten ring nut (2) to 146 ft.-lb. (20 mkg).

It is possible to install suspension unit springs with different characteristics. Soft, standard, and hard springs are available. To replace this spring, proceed as follows.

1. Remove Monocross suspension unit.

2. Cover diaphragm housing bolt holes with rags, then clamp unit in a vise.

3. Remove spring retaining nut and its related hardware.

4. Lift off spring.

5. Reverse the removal procedure to install the new spring. Upon installation, tighten its nut to 11 ft.-lb. (1.5 mkg).

Swinging Arm

Occasionally check for play in swinging arm bushings. To do so, remove the rear wheel and both shock absorbers or Monocross suspension unit. Then shake the swinging arm from side to side. If there is noticeable play, replace the swinging arm bushings and/or shaft. On models used primarily for street riding, these bushings should be replaced at 6,000-mile (10,000-kilometer) intervals. Models used for competition will require replacement at more frequent intervals. Need for replacement may be indicated by shimmy, wander, or rear wheel hop.

1. Remove chaincase mounting bolts.

2. Remove shaft nut, then pull out shaft.

3. Remove old bushings.

4. Reverse the removal procedure to install new bushings.

DRIVE CHAIN

The drive chain is subject to wear and abrasion, and as such, it must be cleaned frequently, lubricated, and adjusted if it is to provide long service.

Cleaning and Lubrication

1. Disconnect master link, then remove chain from motorcycle.

2. Immerse chain in cleaning solvent, and allow it to soak for about ½ hour. Move it around and

flex it during this period so that dirt between pins and rollers can work its way out.

3. Scrub rollers and side plates with a stiff brush, then rinse chain in clean solvent to carry away loosened dirt. Hang chain and allow to dry thoroughly.

4. Lubricate chain with a good grade of chain lubricant, carefully following the lubricant manufacturer's instructions.

5. Reinstall chain on motorcycle. Use a new master link clip and install it in the direction shown in **Figure 37**.

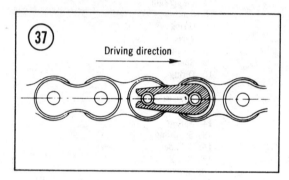

Driving direction

Chain Inspection

1. Refer to **Figure 38**. Replace the chain if it can be pulled away from the rear sprocket more than ½ the length of a link.

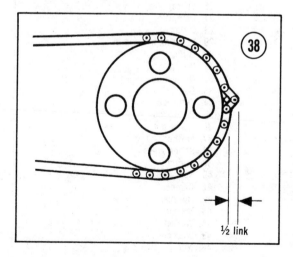

½ link

2. Check for binding links. To do so, hang the chain by one end. If there are any binding links, the chain will exhibit a kink at that point. If cleaning and lubrication does not help the problem, replace the chain.

3. Rust results in rapid wear of pins and rollers. If rust is present, clean and lubricate the chain at once.

Chain Adjustment

When the drive chain is properly adjusted, vertical play in the lower chain run will be approximately ¾-1 in. (20-25mm). If adjustment is required, proceed as follows.

1. Loosen rear axle locknut. On models with rubber rear hub dampers, there is an additional nut which must be loosened.

2. Loosen both chain adjuster locknuts, then turn both chain adjusters as required to adjust chain free play.

3. Refer to **Figure 39**. Note that there is an alignment mark on each chain adjuster, and several marks on each swing arm. The alignment mark on each chain adjuster must align with corresponding swing arm marks. For example, if the left chain adjuster aligns with the third swing arm mark from the front, the right chain adjuster must align with the third mark from the front. Turn either adjuster as required until this condition exists.

4. Recheck chain free play, and readjust if required by turning both chain adjusters an equal amount.

5. Tighten axle nut and chain adjuster locknuts.

6. Chain adjustment may affect rear brake adjustment. Adjust the rear brake if necessary.

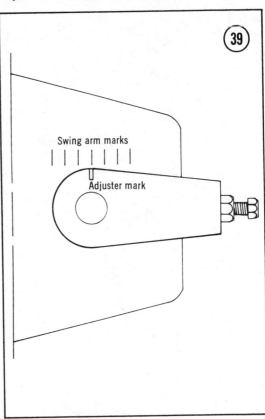

Swing arm marks

Adjuster mark

7

APPENDIX I

SPECIFICATIONS

This section contains specifications and performance figures for the various models covered by this book. The tables are arranged in order of increasing engine displacement. Since there are differences between various models, be sure to consult the correct table for the motorcycle in question.

DT1 AND DT1-B

Dimensions	
Overall length	81.1 in.
Overall width	35.0 in.
Wheelbase	53.6 in.
Ground clearance	9.6 in.
Weight	232 lb.
Engine	
Displacement	246cc
Bore x stroke	70x64mm
Compression ratio	6.8:1
Torque, ft.-lb./rpm	16.8/5,000
Lubrication system	Autolube
Ignition system	Magneto
Tire size	
Front	3.25-19
Rear	4.00-18

DT1C-MX AND DT1-MX

Dimensions	
Overall length	——
Overall width	——
Wheelbase	——
Ground clearance	——
Weight	229 lb.
Engine	
Displacement	246cc
Bore x stroke	70x64mm
Compression ratio	8.2:1
Torque, ft.-lb./rpm	22.4/6,500
Lubrication system	Autolube
Ignition system	Magneto
Tire size	
Front	2.75-21
Rear	4.00-18

DT1-C

Dimensions	
Overall length	81.1 in.
Overall width	35.0 in.
Wheelbase	53.6 in.
Ground clearance	9.6 in.
Weight	240 lb.
Engine	
Displacement	246cc
Bore x stroke	70x64mm
Compression ratio	6.4:1
Torque, ft.-lb./rpm	17.5/6,500
Lubrication system	Autolube
Ignition system	Magneto
Tire size	
Front	3.25-19
Rear	4.00-18

DT1-E

Dimensions	
Overall length	82.7 in.
Overall width	35.0 in.
Wheelbase	54.7 in.
Ground clearance	10.0 in.
Weight	245 lb.
Engine	
Displacement	246cc
Bore x stroke	70 x 64mm
Compression ratio	6.8:1
Torque, ft.-lb./rpm	17.5/6,500
Lubrication system	Autolube
Ignition system	Magneto
Tire size	
Front	3.25-19
Rear	4.00-18

DT2 AND DT3

Dimensions

Overall length	82.7 in.
Overall width	35.0 in.
Wheelbase	54.7 in.
Ground clearance	10.0 in.

Weight   258 lb.

Engine

Displacement	246cc
Bore x stroke	70x64mm
Compression ratio	6.8:1
Torque, ft.-lb./rpm	18.3/6,000

Lubrication system   Autolube

Ignition system   Magneto

Tire size

Front	3.25-19
Rear	4.00-18

MX250

Dimensions

Overall length	83.1 in.
Overall width	37.4 in.
Wheelbase	55.9 in.
Ground clearance	8.9 in.

Weight   227 lb.

Engine

Displacement	246cc
Bore x stroke	70x64mm
Compression ratio	7.4:1
Torque, ft.-lb./rpm	21.9/7,000

Lubrication system   Autolube

Ignition system   Magneto

Tire size

Front	3.00-21
Rear	4.00-21

DT2-MX

Dimensions

Overall length	82.7 in.
Overall width	35.0 in.
Wheelbase	54.7 in.
Ground clearance	10.0 in.

Weight   224 lb.

Engine

Displacement	246cc
Bore x stroke	70x64mm
Compression ratio	7.1:1
Torque, ft.-lb./rpm	20.7/7,000

Lubrication system   Autolube

Ignition system   Magneto

Tire size

Front	3.00-21
Rear	4.00-18

YZ250

Dimensions

Overall length	83.1 in.
Overall width	35.0 in.
Wheelbase	55.9 in.
Ground clearance	8.9 in.

Weight   207 lb.

Engine

Displacement	246cc
Bore x stroke	70x64mm
Compression ratio	7.4:1
Torque, ft.-lb./rpm	———

Lubrication system   Gas-oil mixture

Ignition system   Magneto

Tire size

Front	3.00-21
Rear	4.00-18

8

DT250

Dimensions

Overall length	46.46 in.
Overall width	34.3 in.
Wheelbase	55.7 in.
Ground clearance	7.9 in.

Weight   265 lb.

Engine

Displacement	246cc
Bore x stroke	70x64mm
Compression ratio	——
Torque, ft.-lb./rpm	——

Lubrication system   Autolube

Ignition system   Magneto

Tire size

Front	3.00-21
Rear	4.00-18

RT1-MX AND RT1B-MX

Dimensions

Overall length	82.7 in.
Overall width	35.0 in.
Wheelbase	54.7 in.
Ground clearance	10.0 in.

Weight   258 lb.

Engine

Displacement	351cc
Bore x stroke	80x70mm
Compression ratio	7.2:1
Torque, ft.-lb./rpm	28.7/6,500

Lubrication system   Autolube

Ignition system   Magneto

Tire size

Front	2.75-21
Rear	4.00-18

RT1 AND RT1-B

Dimensions

Overall length	82.7 in.
Overall width	35.0 in.
Wheelbase	54.7 in.
Ground clearance	10.0 in.

Weight   258 lb.

Engine

Displacement	351cc
Bore x stroke	80x70mm
Compression ratio	6.3:1
Torque, ft.-lb./rpm	26.0/5,500

Lubrication system   Autolube

Ignition system   Magneto

Tire size

Front	3.25-19
Rear	4.00-18

RT2 AND RT3

Dimensions

Overall length	82.7 in.
Overall width	35.0 in.
Wheelbase	54.7 in.
Ground clearance	10.0 in.

Weight   262 lb.

Engine

Displacement	351cc
Bore x stroke	80x70mm
Compression ratio	6.3:1
Torque, ft.-lb./rpm	27.7/5,500

Lubrication system   Autolube

Ignition system   Magneto

Tire size

Front	3.25-19
Rear	4.00-18

RT2-MX

Dimensions

Overall length	82.7 in.
Overall width	35.0 in.
Wheelbase	54.7 in.
Ground clearance	10.0 in.

Weight   227 lb.

Engine

Displacement	351cc
Bore x stroke	80x70mm
Compression ratio	7.1:1
Torque, ft.-lb./rpm	27.7/7,000

Lubrication system   Autolube

Ignition system   CDI

Tire size

Front	3.00-21
Rear	4.00-18

MX360A

Dimensions

Overall length	83.1 in.
Overall width	37.4 in.
Wheelbase	55.9 in.
Ground clearance	8.9 in.

Weight   234 lb.

Engine

Displacement	351cc
Bore x stroke	80x70mm
Compression ratio	——
Torque, ft.-lb./rpm	——

Lubrication system   Autolube

Ignition system   CDI

Tire size

Front	3.00-21
Rear	4.00-18

MX360

Dimensions

Overall length	83.1 in.
Overall width	37.4 in.
Wheelbase	55.9 in.
Ground clearance	8.9 in.

Weight   234 lb.

Engine

Displacement	351cc
Bore x stroke	80x70mm
Compression ratio	7.0:1
Torque, ft.-lb./rpm	28.0/7,000

Lubrication system   Autolube

Ignition system   CDI

Tire size

Front	3.00-21
Rear	4.00-18

YZ360

Dimensions

Overall length	83.1 in.
Overall width	35.0 in.
Wheelbase	55.9 in.
Ground clearance	8.9 in.

Weight   212 lb.

Engine

Displacement	351cc
Bore x stroke	80x70mm
Compression ratio	7.0:1
Torque, ft.-lb./rpm	——

Lubrication system   Gas-oil mixture

Ignition system   CDI

Tire size

Front	3.00-21
Rear	4.60-18

8

DT360

Dimensions	
Overall length	85.8 in.
Overall width	34.3 in.
Wheelbase	56.1 in.
Ground clearance	8.7 in.
Weight	276 lb.
Engine	
Displacement	351cc
Bore x stroke	80x70mm
Compression ratio	——
Torque, ft.lb./rpm	——
Lubrication system	Autolube
Ignition system	CDI
Tire size	
Front	3.00-21
Rear	4.00-18

DT400

Dimensions	
Overall length	85.8 in.
Overall width	34.3 in.
Wheelbase	55.5 in.
Ground clearance	8.7 in.
Weight	272 lb.
Engine	
Displacement	397cc
Bore x stroke	85x70mm
Compression ratio	6.4:1
Torque, ft.-lb./rpm	27.5/5,000
Lubrication system	Autolube
Ignition system	CDI
Tire size	
Front	3.00-21
Rear	4.00-18

INDEX

9

YAMAHA 250-500cc SINGLES
Supplement for United Kingdom

This supplement points out special features of bikes delivered to the United Kingdom.

LUBRICANTS AND PETROL

U.K. models use the same lubricants and petrol as U.S. models. **Table 1** indicates recommended types and capacities in Imperial measure.

HEADLAMP

United Kingdom models use a prefocused headlamp bulb and a city (pilot) lamp.

Headlamp Bulb Replacement

1. Remove the headlamp retaining screw and gently pry off the headlamp rim and reflector unit (**Figure 1**).

Table 1   RECOMMENDED LUBRICANTS AND PETROL

	Capacity	Type
Engine oil	2¾ Imp. pt.	SAE 30 2-stroke engine oil
Transmission oil		SAE 10W/30 engine oil
250 (through 1973)	1000cc	
250 (1974 and later)	1200cc	
360 (1974 and later)	1200cc	
400	1000cc	
Front forks		
DT1, DT1-B, DT1-C	210cc	SAE 10W/30 engine oil;
DT1-E, DT1E-MX	175cc	SAE 30 or 40 for hot
DT2, DT2-MX	175cc	weather or severe use
DT3, MX250, DT250A	175cc	
MX250A, YZ250A	195cc	
RT1, RT1-MX	210cc	
RT1B, RT1B-MX	175cc	
RT2, RT2-MX	175cc	
RT3	175cc	
MX360	195cc	
YZ360A	195cc	
DT400C	175cc	
YZ250/400	338cc	
IT250/400	250cc	
DT250/400	190.5cc	
Fuel	2.0 Imp. gal.	85 octane or higher
Brake fluid	—	J-1703

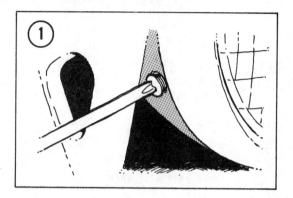

2. The bulb is held in place in the rear of the reflector by a rubber boot (**Figure 2**). Remove this boot and then remove the bulb (**Figure 3**). Note that the bulb is located with 3 pins.

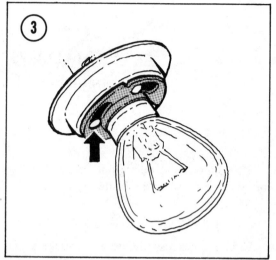

3. Install a new bulb by reversing the preceding steps.

City (Pilot) Lamp Replacement

1. The pilot bulb is held in place in the reflector by a rubber boot (**Figure 4**). Remove this boot and pull the pilot bulb holder out.

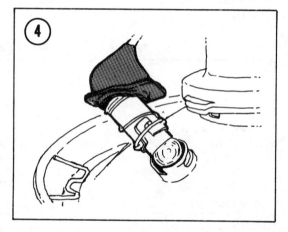

2. Remove the bulb from the holder by twisting gently and pulling it out.

3. Install a new pilot bulb by reversing the preceding steps.

BULB TYPES

Table 2 lists bulbs used in United Kingdom models.

Table 2   BULB TYPES

Application	Rating
Headlamp	35W/35W
Tail/stop lamp	5.3W/17W
Turn signal lamps	17W
City (pilot) lamp	1.5W
Instrument lamps	3W

NOTES

NOTES